Java 1.5 Tiger

A Developer's Notebook™

Java 1.5 Tiger

A Developer's Notebook™

Brett McLaughlin and David Flanagan

O'REILLY®

Beijing · Cambridge · Farnham · Köln · Paris · Sebastopol · Taipei · Tokyo

Java 1.5 Tiger: A Developer's Notebook™
by Brett McLaughlin and David Flanagan

Published by O'Reilly Media, Inc., 1005 Gravenstein Highway North, Sebastopol, CA 95472.

O'Reilly books may be purchased for educational, business, or sales promotional use. Online editions are also available for most titles (*safari.oreilly.com*). For more information, contact our corporate/institutional sales department: (800) 998-9938 or *corporate@oreilly.com*.

Editor:	Brett McLaughlin
Production Editor:	Reg Aubry
Cover Designer:	Edie Freedman
Interior Designer:	Melanie Wang

Printing History:

June 2004:	First Edition.

RepKover.™ This book uses RepKover™, a durable and flexible lay-flat binding.

ISBN: 0-596-00738-8
[M]

Contents

The Developer's Notebook Series

So, you've managed to pick this book up. Cool. Really, I'm excited about that! Of course, you may be wondering why these books have the odd-looking, college notebook sort of cover. I mean, this is O'Reilly, right? Where are the animals? And, really, do you *need* another series? Couldn't this just be a cookbook? How about a nutshell, or one of those cool hacks books that seems to be everywhere? The short answer is that a developer's notebook is none of those things—in fact, it's such an important idea that we came up with an entirely new look and feel, complete with cover, fonts, and even some notes in the margin. This is all a result of trying to get something into your hands you can actually use.

It's my strong belief that while the nineties were characterized by everyone wanting to learn everything (Why not? We all had six-figure incomes from dot-com companies), the new millennium is about information pain. People don't have time (or the income) to read through 600 page books, often learning 200 things, of which only about 4 apply to their current job. It would be much nicer to just sit near one of the uber-coders and look over his shoulder, wouldn't it? To ask the guys that are neck-deep in this stuff why they chose a particular method, how they performed this one tricky task, or how they avoided that threading issue when working with piped streams. The thinking has always been that books can't serve that particular need—they can inform, and let you decide, but ultimately a coder's mind was something that couldn't really be captured on a piece of paper.

This series says that assumption is patently wrong—and we aim to prove it.

A Developer's Notebook is just what it claims to be: the often-frantic scribbling and notes that a true-blue alpha geek mentally makes when working with a new language, API, or project. It's the no-nonsense code that solves problems, stripped of page-filling commentary that often serves more as a paperweight than an epiphany. It's hackery, focused not on what is nifty or might be fun to do when you've got some free time (when's the last time that happened?), but on what you need to simply "make it work." This isn't a lecture, folks—it's a lab. If you want a lot of concept, architecture, and UML diagrams, I'll happily and proudly point you to our animal and nutshell books. If you want every answer to every problem under the sun, our omnibus cookbooks are killer. And if you are into arcane and often quirky uses of technology, hacks books simply rock. But if you're a coder, down to your core, and you just want to get on with it, then you want a Developer's Notebook. Coffee stains and all, this is from the mind of a developer to yours, barely even cleaned up enough for print. I hope you enjoy it...we sure had a good time writing them.

Notebooks Are...

Example-driven guides

As you'll see in the "Organization" section, developer's notebooks are built entirely around example code. You'll see code on nearly every page, and it's code that *does something*—not trivial "Hello World!" programs that aren't worth more than the paper they're printed on.

Aimed at developers

Ever read a book that seems to be aimed at pointy-haired bosses, filled with buzzwords, and feels more like a marketing manifesto than a programming text? We have too—and these books are the antithesis of that. In fact, a good notebook is incomprehensible to someone who can't program (don't say we didn't warn you!), and that's just the way it's supposed to be. But for developers...it's as good as it gets.

Actually enjoyable to work through

Do you really have time to sit around reading something that isn't any fun? If you do, then maybe you're into thousand-page language references—but if you're like the rest of us, notebooks are a much better fit. Practical code samples, terse dialogue centered around practical examples, and even some humor here and there—these are the ingredients of a good developer's notebook.

About doing, not talking about doing

If you want to read a book late at night without a computer nearby, these books might not be that useful. The intent is that you're coding as you go along, knee deep in bytecode. For that reason, notebooks talk code, code, code. Fire up your editor before digging in.

Notebooks Aren't...

Lectures

We don't let just anyone write a developer's notebook—you've got to be a bona fide programmer, and preferably one who stays up a little too late coding. While full-time writers, academics, and theorists are great in some areas, these books are about programming in the trenches, and are filled with instruction, not lecture.

Filled with conceptual drawings and class hierarchies

This isn't a nutshell (there, we said it). You won't find 100-page indices with every method listed, and you won't see full-page UML diagrams with methods, inheritance trees, and flow charts. What you will find is page after page of source code. Are you starting to sense a recurring theme?

Long on explanation, light on application

It seems that many programming books these days have three, four, or more chapters before you even see any working code. I'm not sure who has authors convinced that it's good to keep a reader waiting this long, but it's not anybody working on *this* series. We believe that if you're not coding within ten pages, something's wrong. These books are also chock-full of practical application, taking you from an example in a book to putting things to work on your job, as quickly as possible.

Organization

Developer's Notebooks try to communicate different information than most books, and as a result, are organized differently. They do indeed have chapters, but that's about as far as the similarity between a notebook and a traditional programming book goes. First, you'll find that all the headings in each chapter are organized around a specific task. You'll note that we said *task*, not *concept*. That's one of the important things to get about these books—they are first and foremost about doing something. Each of these headings represents a single *lab*. A lab is just what it sounds like—steps to accomplish a specific goal. In fact, that's the first heading you'll see under each lab: "How do I do that?" This is the central question of each lab, and you'll find lots of down-and-dirty code and detail in these sections.

Some labs have some things not to do (ever played around with potassium in high school chemistry?), helping you avoid common pitfalls. Some labs give you a good reason for caring about the topic in the first place; we call this the "Why do I care?" section, for obvious reasons. For those times when code samples don't clearly communicate what's going on, you'll find a "What just happened" section. It's in these sections that you'll find concepts and theory—but even then, they are tightly focused on the task at hand, not explanation for the sake of page count. Finally, many labs offer alternatives, and address common questions about different approaches to similar problems. These are the "What about..." sections, which will help give each task some context within the programming big picture.

And one last thing—on many pages, you'll find notes scrawled in the margins of the page. These aren't for decoration; they contain tips, tricks, insights from the developers of a product, and sometimes even a little humor, just to keep you going. These notes represent part of the overall communication flow—getting you as close to reading the mind of the developer-author as we can. Hopefully they'll get you that much closer to feeling like you are indeed learning from a master.

And most of all, remember—these books are...

All Lab, No Lecture

—Brett McLaughlin, Series Creator

Preface

Professional Java
Enterprise Java
Commercial Java

These are all terms that are commonplace in programming discussions these days—and for good reason. Gone are the days when Java was considered a toy language for creating web games, futilely trying to catch up to its "big brothers," C and C++. While AWT and Swing (and now SWT) are important parts of the Java language, Java has also evolved to take on more far-ranging tasks—database interaction, financial management, e-commerce, and more. Its speed is comparable to C, and its APIs are far-reaching. As a result, the core language has undergone significant stabilization, and Java 1.3, and then 1.4, were largely steps towards maturing the platform, rather than radically changing it.

Enter Java 1.5—code-named Tiger. Actually, it's Java 5, version 1.5. Well, it's the J2SE, which I suppose makes it Java 2, Standard Edition, 5, version 1.5. Confusing enough for you? Thankfully, whatever the thing is called, the additions are worthy of all the hubbub; this isn't your father's Java (or to be more accurate, it's not your slightly older brother's Java) anymore.

Looking more like a completely new product than just a revision of an older language, Tiger is chock-full of dramatic changes to what you know as simply Java. You can't just read through the release notes and figure this one out; and since the new features are a lot more important than all the oddities about its versioning, I'll just call it Tiger throughout the book, and sidestep Java 2 version 5...er...version 1.5...well...as I said, Tiger.

Whatever Tiger ends up being called officially, it introduces so many new features to the language that it took nearly 200 pages to cover them— and you'll find that each page of this book is dense with code, example, and terse explanation. There isn't any wasted space. In fact, that's precisely what you're holding in your hands—a concise crash course in the next evolution of Java, Tiger. By the time you're through, you'll be typing your lists, taking your overloading to an entirely new level, writing compile-time checked annotations, and threading more efficiently than ever. And that doesn't take into account how much fun it is to type all sorts of new characters into your source code. You haven't lived until @, <, >, and % are strewn throughout your editor...well, maybe that's just me wanting to have a little more fun at the workplace. Whatever your reason for getting into Tiger, though, you'll find more tools at your disposal than ever before, and far more change in any version of Java since its initial 1.0 release. Fire up your code editor, buckle your seat belts, and get ready to hit the ground running.

Let's tame the Tiger.

Organization

This book is set up to be something of a cross between a learning exercise (where you would read from front to back), and a cookbook (where you can skip around without concern). For the most part, you can feel free to look through the table of contents or index, and find what you're looking for. However, as many of the subjects in this book are interrelated (such as generics, the for/in statement, and autoboxing), you may find yourself reading an article that assumes knowledge from a previous section of the book. In these cases, just browse the referenced chapter, and you should be all set. A little extra learning is a good thing anyway, right?

How This Book Was Written

This book is the result of an unusual, but fruitful collaboration between David Flanagan and Brett McLaughlin. David was at work on the fifth edition of Java in a Nutshell, but was eager to get coverage of the major language changes in Tiger out sooner than the production schedule for that book allowed. Brett, meanwhile, was the driving editorial force behind this innovative new series of Developer's Notebooks, and was eager to include a title on Tiger in the series.

The process went like this:

- David researched the new features of Tiger and wrote about them for Java in a Nutshell. He sent drafts of his new material to Brett.
- Brett feverishly ripped those chapters apart, rewrote almost everything, added new examples, and reassembled everything into the Developer's Notebook format.

The result is a book almost entirely written by Brett, based on research done by David. The tone of the writing and the engaging style of the book is Brett's, and readers of this book and Java in a Nutshell will be hard-pressed to find any duplication of prose. In a few cases, Brett has used code samples that also appear in Java in a Nutshell, and in each case that fact is mentioned in the margin.

About the Examples

This book has hundreds of code examples, spread throughout its pages. While some complete code listings are shown in the text, other examples are shown only in part. While some readers may enjoy typing in these programs on their own, many of us just don't have the time. Because of this, every single example, and almost all of the partial examples, are ready for compilation in Java source files, ready for download.

Additionally, the process of compilation (especially class path issues) remains one of Java's most problematic features. To help you out, an Ant buildfile is included with the samples, called *build.xml*. You'll need to download and install Ant (available at *http://ant.apache.org*) to take advantage of this buildfile, and I strongly urge you to do just that. Ant installation is easy, and you can always refer to *Ant: The Definitive Guide* (O'Reilly) if you need assistance. Your directory structure should look something like this:

```
<basedir>
  |
  +--src (contains build.xml)
  |
  +--classes
```

TIP

This is all taken care of for you if you just download the code and unzip it.

Navigate to your local *src* directory, and type ant. You'll get an error if you don't have Ant set up properly. Otherwise, you should see something like the following:

```
${basedir}\code\src>ant
Buildfile: build.xml

compile:
     [echo] Compiling all Java files...
    [javac] Compiling 41 source files to code\classes
    [javac] Note: code\src\com\oreilly\tiger\ch06\DeprecatedTester.java
                   uses or overrides a deprecated API.
    [javac] Note: Recompile with -Xlint:deprecation for details.
    [javac] Note: Some input files use unchecked or unsafe operations.
    [javac] Note: Recompile with -Xlint:unchecked for details.

BUILD SUCCESSFUL
Total time: 9 seconds
```

I'll leave it to you to explore the other targets within *build.xml*; there are also notes in most chapters about targets that apply to that chapter, or to a specific example. All this code is heavily tested, and mildly documented. Just make sure you've got Tiger as the first Java compiler on your classpath, or you'll get all sorts of nasty errors!

You may download this sample code, as well as check out errata, view related resources and online articles, and see the latest on this book, at *http://www.oreilly.com/catalog/javaadn/*. Check this site often, as lots of new content may be available as time goes by and we update the examples.

Conventions Used in This Book

Italic is used for:

- Pathnames, filenames, program names, compilers, options, and commands
- New terms where they are defined
- Internet addresses, such as domain names and URLs

Boldface is used for:

- Particular keys on a computer keyboard
- Names of user interface buttons and menus

Constant width is used for:

- Anything that appears literally in a JSP page or a Java program, including keywords, data types, constants, method names, variables, class names, and interface names
- Command lines and options that should be typed verbatim on the screen
- All JSP and Java code listings
- HTML documents, tags, and attributes

Constant width italic is used for:

- General placeholders that indicate that an item is replaced by some actual value in your own program

Constant width bold is used for:

- Text that is typed in code examples by the user

TIP

This icon designates a note, which is an important aside to the nearby text.

WARNING

This icon designates a warning relating to the nearby text.

How to Contact Us

Please address comments and questions concerning this book to the publisher:

O'Reilly Media, Inc.
1005 Gravenstein Highway North
Sebastopol, CA 95472
(800) 998-9938 (in the United States or Canada)
(707) 829-0515 (international or local)
(707) 829-0104 (fax)

We have a web page for this book, where we list errata, examples, or any additional information. You can access this page at:

   http://www.oreilly.com/catalog/javaadn/

To comment or ask technical questions about this book, send email to:

   bookquestions@oreilly.com

For more information about our books, conferences, Resource Centers, and the O'Reilly Network, see our web site at:

   http://www.oreilly.com/

Acknowledgments from Brett

The "I" you see in these pages is me—for better or for worse, I came up with this series, and am thrilled to be able to bring one of the first books in the series to you. But, that leads me to the enormously talented group of folks who made that possible.

There was a time when I loved writing acknowledgements, because I got to thank everybody involved in helping me get through another book. Of course, now I realize that there are so many people I forget to thank, that I'm a little scared...I guess that's the Oscar-acceptance-paranoia working itself out. In any case, any book such as this truly is a tremendous effort by a ton of people, and I couldn't go without at least *trying* to name most of them.

To Mike Loukides, who edits most of my books (this being the exception), and Mike Hendrickson, who's just all-around smart—thanks for paving the way for these new, inventive, cool little notebooks. I think you've done the programming world a real service with them. I need to thank David Flanagan for doing all the heavy lifting; the Sun folks, especially at CAP, for letting me see JDK 1.5 early on; and guys like Hans Bergsten, Bruce Perry, Bob McWhirter, and Steve Holzner for writing good books and letting me spend less time editing than I deserve to.

Finally, in trying to keep things brief (you'll think I'm funny because of that, right?), I owe the biggest debt to my family, as is always the case. My wife, Leigh, only gripes occasionally when I'm working at 9:00 at night. Of course, that's mostly because she's exhausted from chasing the two bits of inspiration I have; my older son, Dean, and my younger son, Robbie. When you guys can read, you'll see your names here, so thank the readers for the college fund, OK?

Acknowledgments from David

Thanks first and foremost to Brett for his enthusiasm, and for working overtime and pulling this book together so quickly. Thanks also to Mike Loukides for supporting the endeavor, and to Deb Cameron, my editor for *Java in a Nutshell*, for allowing me the time to work on it.

What's New?

Even with nearly 200 pages before you, it's going to be awfully tough to cover all of Tiger's new features. Whether it's called Java 1.5, 2.0, Java 5, or something altogether different, this version of Java is an entirely new beast, and has tons of meat to offer.

Rather than waste time on introductory text, this chapter jumps right into some of the "one-off" features that are new for Tiger, and that don't fit into any of the larger chapters. These will get you used to the developer's notebook format if it's new for you, and introduce some cool tools along the way. Then Chapter 2 gets downright serious, as generics are introduced, and from there to the last page, it's a race to cram everything in.

In this chapter:
- *Working With Arrays*
- *Using Queues*
- *Ordering Queues Using Comparators*
- *Overriding Return Types*
- *Taking Advantage of Better Unicode*
- *Adding StringBuilder to the Mix*

Working with Arrays

Tiger has a pretty major overhaul of its collection classes, most of which have to do with generic types and support for the new for/in loop. Without getting into those details yet, you can get some immediate bang for your buck by checking out the java.util.Arrays class, which is chock-full of static utility methods (many of which are new to Tiger).

How do I do that?

The java.util.Arrays class is a set of static methods that all are useful for working with arrays. Most of these methods are particularly helpful if you have an array of numeric primitives, which is what Example 1-1 demonstrates (in varied and mostly useless ways).

Example 1-1. Using the Arrays utility class

```java
package com.oreilly.tiger.ch01;

import java.util.Arrays;
import java.util.List;

public class ArraysTester {

  private int[] ar;

  public ArraysTester(int numValues) {
    ar = new int[numValues];

    for (int i=0; i < ar.length; i++) {
      ar[i] = (1000 - (300 + i));
    }
  }

  public int[] get() {
    return ar;
  }

  public static void main(String[] args) {
    ArraysTester tester = new ArraysTester(50);
    int[] myArray = tester.get();

    // Compare two arrays
    int[] myOtherArray = tester.get().clone();
    if (Arrays.equals(myArray, myOtherArray)) {
      System.out.println("The two arrays are equal!");
    } else {
      System.out.println("The two arrays are not equal!");
    }

    // Fill up some values
    Arrays.fill(myOtherArray, 2, 10, new Double(Math.PI).intValue());
    myArray[30] = 98;

    // Print array, as is
    System.out.println("Here's the unsorted array...");
    System.out.println(Arrays.toString(myArray));
    System.out.println();

    // Sort the array
    Arrays.sort(myArray);

    // print array, sorted
    System.out.println("Here's the sorted array...");
    System.out.println(Arrays.toString(myArray));
    System.out.println();
```

Example 1-1. Using the Arrays utility class (continued)

```java
    // Get the index of a particular value
    int index = Arrays.binarySearch(myArray, 98);
    System.out.println("98 is located in the array at index " + index);

    String[][] ticTacToe = { {"X", "O", "O"},
                             {"O", "X", "X"},
                             {"X", "O", "X"}};
    System.out.println(Arrays.deepToString(ticTacToe));

    String[][] ticTacToe2 = { {"O", "O", "X"},
                              {"O", "X", "X"},
                              {"X", "O", "X"}};

    String[][] ticTacToe3 = { {"X", "O", "O"},
                              {"O", "X", "X"},
                              {"X", "O", "X"}};

    if (Arrays.deepEquals(ticTacToe, ticTacToe2)) {
      System.out.println("Boards 1 and 2 are equal.");
    } else {
      System.out.println("Boards 1 and 2 are not equal.");
    }

    if (Arrays.deepEquals(ticTacToe, ticTacToe3)) {
      System.out.println("Boards 1 and 3 are equal.");
    } else {
      System.out.println("Boards 1 and 3 are not equal.");
    }
  }
}
```

The first method to take note of, at least for Tiger fans, is toString( ). This handles the rather annoying task of printing arrays for you. While this is trivial to write on your own, it's still nice that Sun takes care of it for you now. Here's some program output, showing the effects of Arrays. toString( ) on an array:

```
run-ch01:
    [echo] Running Chapter 1 examples from Tiger: A Developer's Notebook

    [echo] Running ArraysTester...
    [java] The two arrays are equal!
    [java] Here's the unsorted array...
    [java] [700, 699, 3, 3, 3, 3, 3, 3, 3, 3, 690, 689, 688, 687, 686, 685,
684, 683, 682, 681, 680, 679, 678, 677, 676, 675, 674, 673, 672, 671, 98,
669, 668, 667, 666, 665, 664, 663, 662, 661, 660, 659, 658, 657, 656, 655,
654, 653, 652, 651]
```

Running Ant and supplying a target of "run-ch01" automates this.

```
[java] Here's the sorted array...
[java] [3, 3, 3, 3, 3, 3, 3, 3, 98, 651, 652, 653, 654, 655, 656, 657,
658, 659, 660, 661, 662, 663, 664, 665, 666, 667, 668, 669, 671, 672, 673,
674, 675, 676, 677, 678, 679, 680, 681, 682, 683, 684, 685, 686, 687, 688,
689, 690, 699, 700]
```

```
[java] 98 is located in the array at index 8
```

Another similar, but also new, method is `deepToString()`. This method takes in an object array, and prints out its contents, including the contents of any arrays that it might contain. For example:

```java
String[][] ticTacToe = { {"X", "O", "O"},
                         {"O", "X", "X"},
                         {"X", "O", "X"}};
System.out.println(Arrays.deepToString(ticTacToe));
```

Here's the output:

```
[java] [[X, O, O], [O, X, X], [X, O, X]]
```

This starts to really come in handy when you've got three or four levels of arrays, and don't want to take the time to write your own recursion printing routines.

Finally, `Arrays` provides a `deepEquals()` method that compares multi-dimensional arrays:

```java
String[][] ticTacToe = { {"X", "O", "O"},
                         {"O", "X", "X"},
                         {"X", "O", "X"}};
System.out.println(Arrays.deepToString(ticTacToe));

String[][] ticTacToe2 = { {"O", "O", "X"},
                          {"O", "X", "X"},
                          {"X", "O", "X"}};

String[][] ticTacToe3 = { {"X", "O", "O"},
                          {"O", "X", "X"},
                          {"X", "O", "X"}};

if (Arrays.deepEquals(ticTacToe, ticTacToe2)) {
  System.out.println("Boards 1 and 2 are equal.");
} else {
  System.out.println("Boards 1 and 2 are not equal.");
}

if (Arrays.deepEquals(ticTacToe, ticTacToe3)) {
  System.out.println("Boards 1 and 3 are equal.");
} else {
  System.out.println("Boards 1 and 3 are not equal.");
}
```

Chapter 1: What's New?

As expected, the first comparison returns `false`, and the second `true`:

```
[java] Boards 1 and 2 are not equal.
[java] Boards 1 and 3 are equal.
```

What About...

...hash codes? Java 101 dictates that every good `equals()` method should be paired with an equivalent `hashCode()`, and the Arrays class is no exception. Arrays defines both `hashCode()` and `deepHashCode()` methods for just this purpose. I'll leave it to you to play with these, but they are self-explanatory:

```
int hashCode = Arrays.deepHashCode(ticTacToe);
```

Using Queues

Another cool collection addition is the `java.util.Queue` class, for all those occasions when you need FIFO (first-in, first-out) action. Using this class is a breeze, and you'll find it's a nice addition to the already robust Java Collection ...er...collection.

Some queues are LIFO (last-in, first-out).

How do I do that?

The first thing to realize is that proper use of a `Queue` implementation is to *avoid* the standard collection methods `add()` and `remove()`. Instead, you'll need to use `offer()` to add elements. Keep in mind that most queues have a fixed size. If you call `add()` on a full queue, an unchecked exception is thrown—which really isn't appropriate, as a queue being full is a *normal* condition, not an exceptional one. `offer()` simply returns `false` if an element cannot be added, which is more in line with standard queue usage.

In the same vein, `remove()` throws an exception if the queue is empty; a better choice is the new `poll()` method, which returns `null` if there is nothing in the queue. Both methods attempt to remove elements from the head of the queue. If you want the head without removing it, use `element()` or `peek()`. Example 1-2 shows these methods in action.

Example 1-2. Using the Queue interface

```
package com.oreilly.tiger.ch01;

import java.io.IOException;
import java.io.PrintStream;
```

Example 1-2. Using the Queue interface (continued)

```java
import java.util.LinkedList;
import java.util.Queue;

public class QueueTester {

  public Queue q;

  public QueueTester() {
    q = new LinkedList();
  }

  public void testFIFO(PrintStream out) throws IOException {
    q.add("First");
    q.add("Second");
    q.add("Third");

    Object o;
    while ((o = q.poll()) != null) {
      out.println(o);
    }
  }

  public static void main(String[] args) {
    QueueTester tester = new QueueTester();

    try {
      tester.testFIFO(System.out);
    } catch (IOException e) {
      e.printStackTrace();
    }
  }
}
```

In `testFIFO( )`, you can see that the first items into the queue are the first ones out:

```
[echo] Running QueueTester...
[java] First
[java] Second
[java] Third
```

As unexciting as that may seem, that's the bulk of what makes Queue unique—the ordering it provides.

If you're paying attention, you might wonder about this bit of code, though:

```java
public Queue q;

public QueueTester() {
  q = new LinkedList();
}
```

In Tiger, LinkedList has been retrofitted to implement the Queue interface. While you can use it like any other List implementation, it can also be used as a Queue implementation.

What about...

...using a queue in a concurrent programming environment? This is a common usage of a queue, when producer threads are filling the queue, and consumer threads are emptying it. This is more of a threading issue, and so I've left it for Chapter 10—but there is plenty of coverage there.

Ordering Queues Using Comparators

While FIFO is a useful paradigm, there are times when you'll want a queue-like structure, ordered by another metric. This is exactly the purpose of PriorityQueue, another Queue implementation. You provide it a Comparator, and it does the rest.

How do I do that?

PriorityQueue works just as any other Queue implementation, and you don't even need to learn any new methods. Instead of performing FIFO ordering, though, a PriorityQueue orders its items by using the Comparator interface. If you create a new queue and don't specify a Comparator, you get what's called *natural ordering*, which applies to any classes that implement Comparable. For numerical values, for instance, this places highest values, well, highest! Here's an example:

```
PriorityQueue<Integer> pq =
  new PriorityQueue<Integer>(20);

// Fill up with data, in an odd order
for (int i=0; i<20; i++) {
  pq.offer(20-i);
}

// Print out and check ordering
for (int i=0; i<20; i++) {
  System.out.println(pq.poll());
}
```

Since no `Comparator` implementation is given to `PriorityQueue`, it orders the numbers lowest to highest, even though they're not added to the queue in that order. So when peeling off elements, the lowest item comes out first:

```
[echo] Running PriorityQueueTester...
[java] 1
[java] 2
[java] 3
[java] 4
[java] 5
[java] 6
[java] 7
[java] 8
[java] 9
[java] 10
[java] 11
[java] 12
[java] 13
[java] 14
[java] 15
[java] 16
[java] 17
[java] 18
[java] 19
[java] 20
```

However, this queue starts to really come into its own when you provide your own comparator, as shown in Example 1-3. This is done via the constructor, and a custom implementation of `java.util.Comparator`.

Example 1-3. Using a PriorityQueue

```java
package com.oreilly.tiger.ch01;

import java.util.Comparator;
import java.util.PriorityQueue;
import java.util.Queue;

public class PriorityQueueTester {

  public static void main(String[] args) {

    PriorityQueue<Integer> pq =
      new PriorityQueue<Integer>(20,
        new Comparator<Integer>() {
          public int compare(Integer i, Integer j) {
            int result = i%2 - j%2;
            if (result == 0)
              result = i-j;
            return result;
          }
        }
      }
```

Example 1-3. Using a PriorityQueue (continued)

```
    );

    // Fill up with data, in an odd order
    for (int i=0; i<20; i++) {
      pq.offer(20-i);
    }

    // Print out and check ordering
    for (int i=0; i<20; i++) {
      System.out.println(pq.poll());
    }
  }
}
```

The output from this is lowest to highest even numbers, and then lowest to highest odd numbers:

```
[echo] Running PriorityQueueTester...
[java] 2
[java] 4
[java] 6
[java] 8
[java] 10
[java] 12
[java] 14
[java] 16
[java] 18
[java] 20
[java] 1
[java] 3
[java] 5
[java] 7
[java] 9
[java] 11
[java] 13
[java] 15
[java] 17
[java] 19
```

Overriding Return Types

One of the most annoying features when you're using Java inheritance is the inability to override return types. This is most commonly desired when you've got a base class, and then a subclass adds a dimension (either literally or figuratively) to the base class. Typically, you're unable to return that extra dimension without defining a new method (and new name), since the method that the base class used probably had a narrower return type. Thankfully, you can solve this problem using Tiger.

How do I do that?

Example 1-4 is a simple class hierarchy that demonstrates overriding the return type of a superclass's method.

Example 1-4. Overriding the methods of a superclass

Keep in mind that none of this code compiles under Java 1.4, or even in Tiger without the "-source 1.5" switch

```
class Point2D {
  protected int x, y;

  public Point2D() {
    this.x=0;
    this.y=0;
  }

  public Point2D(int x, int y) {
    this.x = x;
    this.y = y;
  }
}

class Point3D extends Point2D {
  protected int z;

  public Point3D(int x, int y) {
    this(x, y, 0);
  }

  public Point3D(int x, int y, int z) {
    this.x = x;
    this.y = y;
    this.z = z;
  }
}

class Position2D {
  Point2D location;

  public Position2D() {
    this.location = new Point2D();
  }

  public Position2D(int x, int y) {
    this.location = new Point2D(x, y);
  }

  public Point2D getLocation() {
    return location;
  }
}
```

Example 1-4. Overriding the methods of a superclass (continued)

```
class Position3D extends Position2D {
  Point3D location;

  public Position3D(int x, int y, int z) {
    this.location = new Point3D(x, y, z);
  }

  public Point3D getLocation() {
    return location;
  }
}
```

The key is the line public `Point3D getLocation( )`, which probably looks pretty odd to you, but get used to it. This is called a *covariant return*, and is only allowed if the return type of the subclass is an extension of the return type of the superclass. In this case, this is satisfied by Point3D extending Point2D. It's accomplished through the annotation, covered in detail in Chapter 6.

Taking Advantage of Better Unicode

While many of the features in this chapter and the rest of the book focus on entirely new features, there are occasions where Tiger has simply evolved. The most significant of these is Unicode support. In pre-Tiger versions of Java, Unicode 3.0 was supported, and all of these Unicode characters fit into 16 bits (and therefore a char). Things are different, now, so you'll need to understand a bit more.

How do I do that?

In Tiger, Java has moved to support Unicode 4.0, which defines several characters that don't fit into 16 bits. This means that they won't fit into a char, and that has some far-reaching consequences. You'll have to use int to represent these characters, and as a result methods like Character.isUpperCase( ) and Character.isWhitespace( ) now have variants that accept int arguments. So if you're needing values in Unicode 3.0 that are *not* available in Unicode 3.0, you'll need to use these new methods..

Most of the new characters in Unicode 4.0 are Han ideographs.

What just happened?

To really grasp all this, you have to understand a few basic terms:

codepoint
> A codepoint is a number that represents a specific character. As an example, 0x3C0 is the codepoint for the symbol π.

Basic Multilingual Plan (BMP)
> The BMP is all Unicode codepoints from \u0000 through \uFFFF. All of these codepoints fit into a Java `char`.

supplementary characters
> These are the Unicode codepoints that fall outside of the BMP. There are 21-bit codepoints, with hex values from 010000 through 10FFFF, and must be represented by an `int`.

A `char`, then, represents a BMP Unicode codepoint. To get all the supplementary characters in addition to the BMP, you need to use an `int`. Of course, only the lowest 21 bits are used, as that's all that is needed; the upper 21 bits are zeroed out.

This all applies to "StringBuffer" and "String-Builder" as well.

All this assumes that you're dealing with these characters in isolation, though, and that's hardly the only use-case. More often, you've got to use these characters within the context of a larger `String`. In those situations, an `int` doesn't fit, and instead two `char` values are encoded, and called a *surrogate pair* when linked like this. The first `char` is from the *high-surrogates* range (\uD800-\uDBFF), and the second `char` is from the *low-surrogates* range (\uDC00-\uDFFF). The net effect is that the number of `chars` in a `String` is *not* guaranteed to be the number of codepoints. Sometimes two `chars` represent a single codepoint (Unicode 4.0), and sometimes they represent two codepoints (Unicode 3.0).

Adding StringBuilder to the Mix

As you work through this book, you'll find that in several instances, the class `StringBuilder` is used, most often in the manner that you're used to seeing `StringBuffer` used. `StringBuilder` is a new Tiger class intended to be a drop-in replacement for `StringBuffer` in cases where thread safety isn't an issue.

How do I do that?

Replace all your `StringBuffer` code with `StringBuilder` code. Really—it's as simple as that. If you're working in a single-thread environment, or in a piece of code where you aren't worried about multiple threads accessing the code, or synchronization, it's best to use StringBuilder instead of StringBuffer. All the methods you are used to seeing on StringBuffer exist for StringBuilder, so there shouldn't be any compilation problems doing a straight search and replace on your code. Example 1-5 is just such an example; I wrote it using StringBuffer, and then did a straight search-and-replace, converting every occurrence of "StringBuffer" with "StringBuilder".

Example 1-5. Replacing StringBuffer with StringBuilder

```
package com.oreilly.tiger.ch01;

import java.util.ArrayList;
import java.util.Iterator;
import java.util.List;

public class StringBuilderTester {

  public static String appendItems(List list) {
    StringBuilder b = new StringBuilder();

    for (Iterator i = list.iterator(); i.hasNext(); ) {
      b.append(i.next())
       .append(" ");
    }

    return b.toString();
  }

  public static void main(String[] args) {
    List list = new ArrayList();
    list.add("I");
    list.add("play");
    list.add("Bourgeois");
    list.add("guitars");
    list.add("and");
    list.add("Huber");
    list.add("banjos");

    System.out.println(StringBuilderTester.appendItems(list));
  }
}
```

You'll see plenty of other code samples using StringBuilder in the rest of this book, so you'll be thoroughly comfortable with the class by book's end.

What about...

...all the new formatting stuff in Tiger, like printf( ) and format( )? StringBuilder, as does StringBuffer, implements Appendable, making it usable by the new Formatter object described in Chapter 9. It really is a drop-in replacement—I promise!

CHAPTER 2

Generics

Without any further ado, I'm going to dive right into the deep end of the pool. More than any other feature, Tiger (or whatever version it ends up being labeled as) brings to the table *generics*. While the name might throw you, generics actually bring a greater degree of type safety to Java than anything you could imagine. It's finally possible to create parameterized types, lists that only accept Strings, and ditch all that annoying class-casting code. Even better, you can limit types that your custom classes and methods accept, removing a huge amount of tedious error-checking and type-checking code.

Additionally, generics are foundational to many of the other features specific to Tiger. Generics have a bearing on varargs, annotations, enumerations, collections, and even some of the new concurrency utilities of the language. While you may want to browse through other parts of this book, you'd do well to take your time and really work through this chapter, lab by lab. There, that's enough introduction for a *few* chapters—let's get to it.

Using Type-Safe Lists

One of Java's greatest strengths is its typing. Everything is an object, and, in fact, every class either explicitly or implicitly descends from Object. This provides a tremendous amount of type-safety—your methods can take Integers, Strings, Lists, Maps, or your own custom objects as parameters, and know at the outset what they'll have to work with.

With all this type-safety, Java has a gaping hole that Tiger finally fills—the ability to create type-safe arrays and lists, ensuring that collections of objects only allow for a certain type to be inserted.

How do I do that?

One of the most annoying tasks in Java is having to cast objects pulled out of a `List`, when you already know what's in the `List` (such as when you fill it yourself, or a trusted source handles populating it):

Generics don't apply to primitive types.

```
List listOfStrings = getListOfStrings();
for (Iterator i = listOfStrings.iterator(); i.hasNext(); ) {
  String item = (String)i.next();

  // Work with that string
}
```

Remove that cast, though—pull out (String)—and you'll get a compiler error:

This particular code sample is in com.oreilly. tiger.ch02. GenericsTester.

```
[javac] Compiling 1 source file to code\classes
[javac] code\src\com\oreilly\tiger\ch02\GenericsTester.java:17:
          incompatible types
[javac] found    : java.lang.Object
[javac] required: java.lang.String
[javac]          String item = i.next();
[javac]                                ^
[javac] Note: code\src\com\oreilly\tiger\ch02\GenericsTester.java uses
          unchecked or unsafe operations.
[javac] Note: Recompile with -Xlint:unchecked for details.
[javac] 1 error
```

No matter how much *you* trust the getListOfStrings() method, the compiler doesn't trust it one bit. It assumes the worst, and if you've ever had anyone else work with you, you realize the compiler is often right more than you are.

Generics let you finally get around this, by limiting the type that a particular `List` will accept:

```
List<String> listOfStrings;
```

While this syntax probably looks pretty odd, it does the trick—listOfStrings can now *only* be populated with `String` instances. You also need to assign it an instance that only accepts the same type:

```
List<String> listOfStrings = new LinkedList<String>();
```

I realize that the syntax just gets weirder, but that's what you have to work with. Angle brackets everywhere! Now you can add `Strings` to this `List`, but you *cannot* add any other type:

Here, and in other output dumps, I've made slight formatting changes to fit things on the printed page.

```
List<String> onlyStrings = new LinkedList<String>();
onlyStrings.add("Legal addition");
onlyStrings.add(new StringBuilder("Illegal Addition"));
onlyStrings.add(25);
```

The compiler will let you know about the problem:

```
[javac] code\src\com\oreilly\tiger\ch02\GenericsTester.java:24:
         cannot find symbol
[javac] symbol  : method add(java.lang.StringBuilder)
[javac] location: interface java.util.List<java.lang.String>
[javac]     onlyStrings.add(new StringBuilder("Illegal Addition"));
[javac]                 ^
[javac] src\com\oreilly\tiger\ch02\GenericsTester.java:25: cannot find
symbol
[javac] symbol  : method add(int)
[javac] location: interface java.util.List<java.lang.String>
[javac]     onlyStrings.add(25);
[javac]                 ^
[javac] Note: code\src\com\oreilly\tiger\ch02\GenericsTester.java uses
         unchecked or unsafe operations.
[javac] Note: Recompile with -Xlint:unchecked for details.
[javac] 2 errors
```

What just happened?

In pre-Tiger versions of Java, the method signature for add( ) in List
looked like this:

```
public boolean add(Object obj);
```

In Tiger, though, things have changed:

```
public boolean add(E o);
```

Before you go looking up E in Javadoc, though, it's just a placeholder. It
indicates that this method declares a type variable (E) and can be parameterized. The entire List class is generic:

```
public interface List<E> extends Collection, Iterable {
```

There's that E again. When you supply a type in the initialization of a
List, you *parameterize* the type—you indicate what type its parameters
can accept:

```
List<String> onlyStrings = new LinkedList<String>( );
```

One way to understand this is to imagine that the compiler replaces
every occurrence of E with the type you supplied—in this case, a String.
Of course, this is just done for this particular instance of List. You can
have multiple Lists, all with different types, and all in the same program block.

The end result of all this is that onlyStrings no longer has a method
add(Object obj); it only has add(String o). So, when the compiler sees
add( ) with anything other than a String parameter, it kicks out an error.
This is the power of generics, and parameterized types—they provide
built-in type safety for your collection types.

What about...

...lists of primitive types? The types that are allowed by Lists (and other collection classes) are all objects; as a result, they don't work with primitive values. The introduction of generics, despite all of its wonder and magic, doesn't change this. So the following won't compile:

```
List<int> list = new LinkedList<int>();
```

However, this will:

```
List<Integer> list = new LinkedList<Integer>();
```

If you're thinking that now you've got to do all sorts of annoying conversion between int and Integer, that's just because you haven't made it to Chapter 4 yet. In that chapter, you'll see that autoboxing makes this a particularly useful way to deal with primitives.

Using Type-Safe Maps

As cool as generics make the List class, it wouldn't be much good if that was the only collection that could be parameterized. *All* of the various collection classes are now generic types, and accept type parameters. Since most of these behave like List, I'll spare you the boring prose of covering each one. It is worth looking at Map, though, as it takes two type parameters, instead of just one. You use it just as you use List, but with two types at declaration and initialization.

How do I do that?

java.util.Map has a key type (which can be any type) and a value type (which can be any type). While it's common to use a numeric or String key, that's not built into the language, and you can't depend on it—at least, not until Tiger came along:

```
Map<Integer, Integer> squares = new HashMap<Integer, Integer>();

for (int i=0; i<100; i++) {
  squares.put(i, i*i);
}

for (int i=0; i<10; i++) {
  int n = i*3;
  out.println("The square of " + n + " is " + squares.get(n));
}
```

This is a simple example of where a new Map is declared, and both its key and value types are defined as Integer. This ensures that you don't have to do any casting, either in putting values into the Map or pulling them out. Pretty easy stuff, isn't it? Of course, you could use any of the following lines of code as well:

```
// Key and value are Strings
Map<String, String> strings = new HashMap<String, String>();

// Key is a String, value is an Object
Map<String, Object> map = new HashMap<String, Object>();

// Key is a Long, value is a String
Map<Long, String> args = new HashMap<Long, String>();
```

What just happened?

As briefly mentioned in "Using Type-Safe Lists," autoboxing helps when you want to stuff primitives into a collection. In this case, even though the Map is defined to take Integers, it's the int counter i that is used to create values. Without getting into the details covered in Chapter 4, Java autoboxes the int value of i into an Integer, behind the scenes, meeting the requirements of the squares Map.

Iterating Over Parameterized Types

Although the for/in loop provides a means of almost completely avoiding the java.util.Iterator class, that particular feature of Tiger isn't covered until Chapter 7. But until you get to that chapter (and probably occasionally after that), it's still useful to know how generic collection types affect Iterator. You'll need to perform an extra step to get the full power of generics.

How do I do that?

It would seem that once you've parameterized your collections, grabbing an Iterator and using it would be trivial:

```
List<String> listOfStrings = new LinkedList<String>();
listOfStrings.add("Happy");
listOfStrings.add("Birthday");
listOfStrings.add("To");
listOfStrings.add("You");

for (Iterator i = listOfStrings.iterator(); i.hasNext(); ) {
   String s = i.next();
   out.println(s);
}
```

However, all is not well. Here's what the compiler spits back to you:

```
[javac] code\src\com\oreilly\tiger\ch02\GenericsTester.java:54:
            incompatible types
[javac] found    : java.lang.Object
[javac] required: java.lang.String
[javac]        String s = i.next();
[javac]                         ^
[javac] Note: code\src\com\oreilly\tiger\ch02\GenericsTester.java
            uses unchecked or unsafe operations.
[javac] Note: Recompile with -Xlint:unchecked for details.
[javac] 1 error
```

The problem here is that while you've parameterized your List, you *haven't* parameterized your Iterator. It's still spitting out Objects, and doesn't know that it should only expect to receive and respond with String types. Just like the collections, Iterator is a generic type in Java, and is declared as public interface Iterator<E>. Its next() method, then, returns E (which is a placeholder, as detailed in "Using Type-Safe Lists"). To parameterize it, you use the same syntax as you did for collection classes:

```
List<String> listOfStrings = new LinkedList<String>();
listOfStrings.add("Happy");
listOfStrings.add("Birthday");
listOfStrings.add("To");
listOfStrings.add("You");

for (Iterator<String> i = listOfStrings.iterator(); i.hasNext(); ) {
  String s = i.next();
  out.println(s);
}
```

Now this Iterator only works with String types, and your code compiles (and runs) normally. You should always pair your Iterators with your collections like this—if the collection is parameterized, the Iterator should use the same parameter.

What about...

...if you define a typesafe Iterator, for a collection that *isn't* typesafe. Well, you're basically playing with fire, and assuming that someone filled the collection correctly. The following code, for example, compiles and runs without a problem (although you'll get lint warnings, detailed in "Checking for Lint":

```
public void testTypeSafeIterators(PrintStream out) throws IOException {
  List listOfStrings = new LinkedList();
  listOfStrings.add("Happy");
  listOfStrings.add("Birthday");
  listOfStrings.add("To");
```

```
        listOfStrings.add("You");

        for (Iterator<String> i = listOfStrings.iterator(); i.hasNext(); ) {
          String s = i.next();
          out.println(s);
        }
    }
```

In this case, it was probably just an oversight that List wasn't also parameterized. However, the following code also compiles fine, but fails horribly at runtime:

```
    public void testTypeSafeIterators(PrintStream out) throws IOException {
      List listOfStrings = getList();

      for (Iterator<String> i = listOfStrings.iterator(); i.hasNext(); ) {
        String s = i.next();
        out.println(s);
      }
    }

    private List getList() {
      List list = new LinkedList();
      list.add(3);
      list.add("Blind");
      list.add("Mice");

      return list;
    }
```

The getList() method, which presumably could have been coded by a trusted (or even a non-trusted) source, is supposed to return only String objects (at least, that's inferred by the use of Iterator<String>). However, it adds a numeric object (an int that gets boxed into an Integer), and at runtime a nasty ClassCastException pops up. This is why you should always parameterize your collections if you want to parameterize your Iterators. If you took that step, you'd get an error at compile-time when trying to assign the List returned from getList() (which is not parameterized) to a List<String>. That error protects you from problems just like this one.

Accepting Parameterized Types as Arguments

So far, all of this parameterization has occurred in the same code block. However, that's unrealistic, and you'll quickly want to write methods that take advantage of parameterized types. This is where generics start to really become powerful. First, you need to understand how a method can tell the compiler that it only accepts a specific parameterization of a generic type.

How do I do that?

Just use the same syntax you've been using (and which should be getting oddly comfortable by this point) in your argument list:

```
private void printListOfStrings(List<String> list, PrintStream out)
  throws IOException {

  for (Iterator<String> i = list.iterator(); i.hasNext(); ) {
    out.println(i.next());
  }
}
```

This allows your method body to act on that parameterization, avoiding class casts and the like. In this example, it's possible to parameterize the Iterator as well, because the compiler ensures that only List<String> is passed into the method. Any other List types are refused (at compile-time).

What about...

...trying to pass in a plain old List, without any parameterization, even if it has only Strings in it? This actually will work, with the caveat that you're left to your own devices in ensuring that the List has in it what it's supposed to. If not, you'll get more ClassCastExceptions than you can shake a stick at, all at runtime. In either case, you'll get lint warnings, which are described in "Checking for Lint," later in this chapter.

Returning Parameterized Types

In addition to accepting parameterized types as arguments, methods in Tiger can return types that are parameterized.

How do I do that?

Remember the getListOfStrings() method, referred to in "Using Type-Safe Lists"? Here is the actual code for that method:

```
private List getListOfStrings() {
  List list = new LinkedList ();
  list.add("Hello");
  list.add("World");
  list.add("How");
  list.add("Are");
```

```
    list.add("You?");

    return list;
}
```

While this is a workable method, it's going to generate all sorts of `lint` warnings (see "Checking for Lint" for details) because it doesn't specify a type for the `List`. Even more importantly, code that uses this method can't assume that it is really getting a `List` of Strings. To correct this, just parameterize the return type, as well as the `List` that is eventually returned by the method:

```
private List<String> getListOfStrings() {
    List<String> list = new LinkedList<String>();
    list.add("Hello");
    list.add("World");
    list.add("How");
    list.add("Are");
    list.add("You?");

    return list;
}
```

Pretty straightforward, isn't it? The return value of this method can now be used immediately in type-safe ways:

```
List<String> strings = getListOfStrings();

for (String s : strings) {
    out.println(s);
}
```

This isn't possible, without compile-time warnings, unless `getListOfStrings()` has a parameterized return value.

Using Parameterized Types as Type Parameters

Collections in Tiger are generic types, and accept type parameters. However, these collections can store collections themselves, which are in turn also generics. This means that a parameterized type can be used as the type parameter to another generic type.

How do I do that?

The `Map` interface takes two type parameters: one for the key, and one for the value itself. While the key is usually a `String` or numeric ID, the value can be anything—including a generic type, like a `List` of Strings.

So `List<String>` becomes a parameterized type, which can be supplied to the `Map` declaration:

```
Map<String, List<String>> map = new HashMap<String, List<String>>();
```

If that's not enough angle brackets for you, here's yet another layer of generics to add into the mix:

```
Map<String, List<List<int[]>>> map = getWeirdMap();
```

Of course, where things get really nuts is actually accessing objects from this collection:

```
int value = map.get(someKey).get(0).get(0)[0];
```

What's cool about this is that all the casting is handled for you—you don't need to do any casting to `List`, but instead can just let the compiler unravel all your parameterized types for you.

Checking for Lint

Several times in this chapter, you've heard about `lint` warnings, which sounds more like something you get out of a dryer than a compiler. These warnings are a new feature of Tiger, though, and important in figuring out how to really bulletproof your code.

How do I do that?

Take a simple piece of code that used a type that can be parameterized, but without type parameters:

```
private List getList() {
    List list = new LinkedList();
    list.add(3);
    list.add("Blind");
    list.add("Mice");

    return list;
}
```

If you compile this in Tiger, with the `-source 1.5` flag, you'll get this message:

```
Note: GenericsTester.java uses unchecked or unsafe operations.
Note: recompile with -Xlint:unchecked for details.
```

If you recompile with the suggested flag, you are telling the compile to show `lint` warnings (-Xlint), and specifically to show those warnings that are unchecked. .

Here's some sample output with these warnings turned on:

```
[javac] code\src\com\oreilly\tiger\ch02\GenericsTester.java:63: warning:
```

You can compile all of the examples for this book with "-Xlint:unchecked" by using the Ant target "compile-check".

```
       [unchecked] unchecked call to add(E) as a member of
       the raw type java.util.List
[javac]     list.add(3);
[javac]          ^
[javac] src\com\oreilly\tiger\ch02\GenericsTester.java:64: warning:
       [unchecked] unchecked call to add(E) as a member of
       the raw type java.util.List
[javac]     list.add("Blind");
[javac]          ^
[javac] src\com\oreilly\tiger\ch02\GenericsTester.java:65: warning:
       [unchecked] unchecked call to add(E) as a member of
       the raw type java.util.List
[javac]     list.add("Mice");
[javac]          ^
[javac] 3 warnings
```

These warnings indicate that the compiler isn't able to ensure that the values added to the list (named `list` in this case) are the intended type. That's because `list` wasn't parameterized.

You can get rid of these warnings by specifying a type in your `List` construction:

```
private List getList() {
    List<Object> list = new LinkedList<Object>();
    list.add(3);
    list.add("Blind");
    list.add("Mice");

    return list;
}
```

Autoboxing is covered in Chapter 4.

While this doesn't do much for type-safety, it does take care of the warnings, as the types being added to `list` are all of type `Object` (the literal 3 is autoboxed to an `Integer`, which is of course an `Object`).

What about...

...annotations? For those of you who may be ahead on Tiger, there is an annotation, called `SuppressWarnings`, which allows you to keep these warnings from showing up in a compilation using `-source 1.5`. You can also just recompile under Java 1.4, although that's obviously a pretty shortsighted solution. The best choice, if at all possible, is to parameterize your generic types, and enforce type-safety whenever possible.

Annotations are covered in Chapter 6.

Generics and Type Conversions

Now that you have all your nifty parameterized types, you'll probably want to perform all sorts of nifty type conversions. This `List` of `Integers` gets tossed into that `Map` of `Numbers`...then again, it's not quite that easy.

You'll need to take great care if you want these conversions to actually work.

How do I do that?

The key in casting generic types is to understand that as with normal, non-generic types, they form a hierarchy. What's unique about generics, though, is that the hierarchy is based on the base type, *not* the parameters to that type. For example, consider this declaration:

```
LinkedList<Float> floatList = new LinkedList<Float>();
```

The conversion is based on LinkedList, *not* Float. So this is legal:

```
List<Float> moreFloats = floatList;
```

However, the following is not:

```
LinkedList<Number> numberList = floatList;
```

While Float is indeed a subclass of Number, it's the generic type that is important, not the parameter type.

What just happened?

There are two key things to understand if you want to know why type conversions work like this; the first is seeing how type conversions can be abused, and the second is erasure. First, consider this sample code, which is actually illegal in Tiger; it demonstrates why converting a LinkedList<Float> to a LinkedList<Number> (or even to a LinkedList<Object>) should indeed be illegal:

```
List<Integer> ints = new ArrayList<Integer>();
ints.add(1);
ints.add(2);

// This is illegal, but use it for illustration purposes
List<Number> numbers = ints;

// Now a float is being added to a list of ints! This results in a
//    ClassCastException when the item is retrieved from the
//    list and used as an int (instead of a float)
numbers.add(1.2);

// This is even worse
List<Object> objects = ints;
objects.add("How are you doing?");
```

Clearly, it needs to be the base type that is considered in type conversions, not the parameter type.

The second concept you'll want to grasp is *erasure*. Generics in Tiger is a compile-time process, and all typing information is handled *at compile-time*. Once the classes are compiled, the typing information is erased (thus the term erasure). Consider the following two declarations:

```
List<String> strings = new LinkedList<String>();
List<Integer> ints = new LinkedList<Integer>();
```

This information is used at compile-time to perform type-checking, but then the typing information is dropped out at runtime. So, to the JVM, these declarations actually become:

```
List strings = new LinkedList();
List ints = new LinkedList();
```

The type parameters are gone, now. With that in mind, consider this (illegal) cast:

```
List<Integer> ints = new LinkedList<Integer>();
List<Number> nums = ints;
```

While this may look OK at compile-time, at runtime there are simply two lists, one trying to be cast to the other—without any type-safety in play at all. Again, then, the compiler does the right thing by using the base type, rather than the parameterized type, for cast checks.

What about...

...defeating type-safety? Well, when you understand the reasons for casting restrictions and erasure, it actually becomes pretty easy to get around type checking. First, for backwards-compatibility, you can always cast a parameterized type to a *raw type*—that is, a generic type with no parameterization:

```
List<Integer> ints = new LinkedList<Integer>();

// We can widen (due to backwards compatibility)
List oldList = ints;

// This line should be illegal, but it happily compiles and runs
oldList.add("Hello");

// Here's the problem!
Integer i = ints.get(0);
```

This obviously leads to a ClassCastException at runtime, but it compiles just fine. You'll get an unchecked warning (if you're compiling under Tiger), but that's it.

You can also use erasure to break type-safety. Remember that at runtime, erasure removes all your parameterization. This means that when you

Some folks get upset that parameterization is only a compile-time thing. A worthy gripe, but something (compile-time checking) is almost always better than nothing.

access parameterized types with reflection, you get the effects of erasure, at compile-time (Example 2-1):

Example 2-1. Breaking type safety with reflection

```
package com.oreilly.tiger.ch02;

import java.util.ArrayList;
import java.util.List;

public class BadIdea {

  private static List<Integer> ints = new ArrayList<Integer>();

  public static void fillList(List<Integer> list) {
    for (Integer i : list) {
      ints.add(i);
    }
  }

  public static void printList() {
    for (Integer i : ints) {
      System.out.println(i);
    }
  }

  public static void main(String[] args) {
    List<Integer> myInts = new ArrayList<Integer>();
    myInts.add(1);
    myInts.add(2);
    myInts.add(3);

    System.out.println("Filling list and printing in normal way...");
    fillList(myInts);
    printList();

    try {
      List list = (List)BadIdea.class.getDeclaredField("ints").get(null);
      list.add("Illegal Value!");
    } catch (Exception e) {
      e.printStackTrace();
    }

    System.out.println("Printing with illegal values in list...");
    printList();
  }
}
```

When list is assigned the reference of the ints List, it does not have the Integer restriction that the ints member variable does. As a result, adding a String value (like "Illegal Value!") is perfectly legal—erasure has removed any parameterization. It's only at runtime, when iterating over the list and printing it, that the problem shows up.

Using Type Wildcards

So now you've got generic types figured out, and even understand all the unchecked warnings your code is generating. Still, here are times when you really *do* want a plain old List, or Map, or whatever, without parameterization. This is going to result in unchecked errors, unless you employ the generics wildcard.

While I'm sure plenty of folks disagree, I think production code shouldn't issue warnings.

How do I do that?

To illustrate the problem, here's a really simple method that prints out all the members of a List:

```
public void printList(List list, PrintStream out) throws IOException {
    for (Iterator i = list.iterator(); i.hasNext(); ) {
        out.println(i.next().toString());
    }
}
```

The problem is that this generates unchecked warnings, something you should avoid whenever possible. What you're really saying, though, is that printList() takes *any* List. This is where the wildcard operator comes in, which for generics is a question mark (?). Make the following change:

Since writing this, later versions of the compiler don't throw warnings here. Still, it makes a good point, so I've left it in for you.

```
public void printList(List<?> list, PrintStream out) throws IOException {
    for (Iterator<?> i = list.iterator(); i.hasNext(); ) {
        out.println(i.next().toString());
    }
}
```

You've now expressed in syntax what you meant—any type is acceptable, and the unchecked warnings go away.

What about...

...using List<Object> to get around this same problem? You might want to review "Generics and Type Conversions," and see if you really want to do that. A List<Integer> *cannot* be passed to a method that takes a List<Object>, remember? So your printList() method would be limited to collections defined as List<Object>, which isn't much use at all. In these cases, the wildcard really is the only viable solution.

You should also be thinking about the declaration of methods in classes like this:

```
public interface List<E> {

    public E get();

    public void add(E value);
}
```

You would read this as a "list of unknown".

Since you've declared the list as a List<?>, get() now returns an Object, which is as close to "unknown" as Java gets. At the same type, this is very different from a List<Object>, which can *only* work with Objects. Where things get even odder is for the add() and other methods that take a parameter that matches the type of the collection. Since the compiler cannot check to ensure type-safety, it rejects any call to add(), addAll(), and set() for a List<?>. In other words, supplying the wildcard to a generic type effectively makes it read-only.

Writing Generic Types

With an arsenal of generic terminology under your belt, you're probably wondering about writing your own generic types. I'm wondering about it, too, so I figure it's worth covering. They're actually pretty simple to write, and you've already got the tools from earlier labs.

How do I do that?

If you need to define some sort of collection, or container, or other custom object that deals directly with another type, generics add a ton of options to your programming toolkit. For example, Example 2-2 is a basic container structure useful mostly for illustrating important generic concepts.

Example 2-2. A basic generic type

```
package com.oreilly.tiger.ch02;

import java.util.ArrayList;
import java.util.List;

public class Box<T> {

    protected List<T> contents;

    public Box() {
        contents = new ArrayList<T>();
    }
```

You can use anything you want for the type parameter, although a single letter is most common.

Example 2-2. A basic generic type (continued)

```java
  public int getSize() {
    return contents.size();
  }

  public boolean isEmpty() {
    return (contents.size() == 0);
  }

  public void add(T o) {
    contents.add(o);
  }

  public T grab() {
    if (!isEmpty()) {
      return contents.remove(0);
    } else
      return null;
  }
}
```

Just as you've seen in Tiger's pre-defined generic types, a single letter is used as the representative for a type parameter.

You create a new instance of this type exactly as you might expect:

```java
Box<String> box = new Box<String>();
```

This effectively replaces all the occurrences of T with String for that specific instance, and suddenly you've got yourself a String Box, so to speak.

What about...

...static variables? Static variables are shared between object instances, but parameterization occurs on a per-instance basis. So you could feasibly have a Box<Integer>, a Box<String>, and a Box<List<Float>>, all with a shared static variable. That variable, then, cannot make assumptions about the typing of any particular instance, as they may be different. It also cannot use a parameterized type—so the following is illegal:

```java
private static List<T> staticList = new ArrayList<T>();
```

You can, however, use static methods that themselves have parameterized types:

```java
public static int biggest(Box<T> box1, Box<U> box2) {
  int box1Size = box1.getSize();
  int box2Size = box2.getSize();
  return Math.max(box1Size, box2Size);
}
```

Restricting Type Parameters

Suppose that you want a version of Box that only accepts numbers—and further, that based on that, you want to add some functionality that's specific to numbers. To accomplish this, you need to restrict the types that are allowed.

How do I do that?

This is pretty simple—you can actually insert an extends *className* onto your type variable, and voila! Check out Example 2-3.

Example 2-3. Restricting the parameterization type

```
package com.oreilly.tiger.ch02;

import java.util.Iterator;

public class NumberBox<N extends Number> extends Box<N> {

  public NumberBox() {
    super();
  }

  // Sum everything in the box
  public double sum() {
    double total = 0;
    for (Iterator<N> i = contents.iterator(); i.hasNext(); ) {
      total = total + i.next().doubleValue();
    }
    return total;
  }
}
```

The only types allowed here are extensions of the class Number (or Number itself). So the following statement is illegal:

```
NumberBox<String> illegal = new NumberBox<String>();
```

The compiler indicates that the *bound* of this type is not met. The bound, of course, is the restriction put upon typing, and that's exactly what the error message indicates:

```
[javac] code\src\com\oreilly\tiger\ch02\GenericsTester.java:118:
        type parameter java.lang.String is not within its bound
[javac]     NumberBox<String> illegal = new NumberBox<String>();
[javac]          ^
[javac] code\src\com\oreilly\tiger\ch02\GenericsTester.java:118:
        type parameter java.lang.String is not within its bound
[javac]     NumberBox<String> illegal = new NumberBox<String>();
[javac]                                      ^
```

You can use this same syntax in method definitions:

```
public static double sum(Box<? extends Number> box1,
                         Box<? extends Number> box2) {
    double total = 0;
    for (Iterator<? extends Number> i = box1.contents.iterator();
         i.hasNext(); ) {
      total = total + i.next().doubleValue();
    }
    for (Iterator<? extends Number> i = box2.contents.iterator();
         i.hasNext(); ) {
      total = total + i.next().doubleValue();
    }
    return total;
}
```

This starts to get a little weird, I realize, but them's the breaks. It gets worse because you have to use the wildcard indicator, and then repeat the expression (? extends Number) in the method body. One way to clean this up is to declare your own type variable inline (and make your syntax even odder):

```
public static <A extends Number> double sum(Box<A> box1,
                                             Box<A> box2) {
    double total = 0;
    for (Iterator<A> i = box1.contents.iterator(); i.hasNext(); ) {
      total = total + i.next().doubleValue();
    }
    for (Iterator<A> i = box2.contents.iterator(); i.hasNext(); ) {
      total = total + i.next().doubleValue();
    }
    return total;
}
```

The portion of the method declaration right before the return value, <A extends Number>, provides a typing variable which is then used throughout the method declaration and body.

What about...

...the other thousand-and-one variations on this theme? I say that only somewhat tongue-in-cheek, to stress that generics are a huge topic unto themselves. In fact, I suspect that there will be at least a few books entirely on generics alone before 2004 has come to a close, and those books will cover far more than this chapter. It's worth knowing that there are ways to extend classes and implement interfaces in your type variables, there are ways to require the *superclass* of a particular object, and a whole lot more.

You can also check out the in-depth chapter on generics in Java in a Nutshell, Fifth Edition (O'Reilly).

Of course, there are ways to juggle knives also, but some things just don't fit into a developer's notebook. You should have more than enough tools to get most of your programming tasks done, and by the time you've got all this mastered, those other books will probably be on bookshelves. So enjoy this, take a deep breath, and turn the page for more Tiger antics.

CHAPTER 3

Enumerated Types

In Java 1.4 and below, there were two basic ways to define new types: through classes and interfaces. For most object-oriented programming, this would seem to be enough. The problem is that there are still some very specific cases where neither is these is sufficient, most commonly when you need to define a finite set of allowed values for a specific data type. For instance, you might want a type called Grade that can only be assigned values of A, B, C, D, F, or Incomplete. Any other values are illegal for this type. This sort of construct is possible prior to Tiger, but it takes a lot of work, and there are still some significant problems.

Since we're good developers and try our best to avoid a lot of work whenever possible, Sun finally helped us out with the new enumerated type (generally referred to simply as an *enum*). This chapter deals with enums: how to create, use, and program with them.

Creating an Enum

Creating an enumerated type involves three basic components, at a minimum:

- The enum keyword
- A name for the new type
- A list of allowed values for the type

There are several optional components that may be defined as well:

- An interface or set of interfaces that the enum implements
- Variable definitions
- Method definitions
- Value-specific class bodies

These optional components are detailed in the labs throughout this chapter; this lab covers the most basic concepts of enumerated types.

Enums allow you to dump most of your "public static final" variable declarations.

How do I do that?

Example 3-1 is about as basic of an enum as you'll find, representing a simple Grade object.

Example 3-1. A simple enumerated type

```
package com.oreilly.tiger.ch03;

public enum Grade { A, B, C, D, F, INCOMPLETE };
```

You can then define a class that refers to this enum just as it would to any other Java class or interface, as shown in Example 3-2.

More often than not, you'll only need the basic enum functionality.

Example 3-2. Referring to an enum in another class

```
package com.oreilly.tiger.ch03;

public class Student {

  private String firstName;
  private String lastName;
  private Grade grade;

  public Student(String firstName, String lastName) {
    this.firstName = firstName;
    this.lastName = lastName;
  }

  public void setFirstName(String firstName) {
    this.firstName = firstName;
  }

  public String getFirstName() {
    return firstName;
  }

  public void setLastName(String lastName) {
    this.lastName = lastName;
  }

  public String getLastName() {
    return lastName;
  }

  public String getFullName() {
    return new StringBuffer(firstName)
        .append(" ")
        .append(lastName)
```

The convention is to use all capital letters for enumerated type identifiers.

"Grade" is used just like any other Java type.

Example 3-2. *Referring to an enum in another class (continued)*

```
          .toString();
  }

  public void assignGrade(Grade grade) {
    this.grade = grade;
  }

  public Grade getGrade() {
    return grade;
  }
}
```

Pretty basic, isn't it? The final piece is actually using this code in conjunction with the enum, as shown here:

```
public void testGradeAssignment(PrintStream out) throws IOException {
  Student student1 = new Student("Brett", "McLaughlin");
  Student student2 = new Student("Ben", "Rochester");
  Student student3 = new Student("Dennis", "Erwin");

  student1.assignGrade(Grade.B);
  student2.assignGrade(Grade.INCOMPLETE);
  student3.assignGrade(Grade.A);
}
```

This code is in the com.oreilly.tiger.ch03.GradeTester class.

I realize that you may have expected some complex treatment of enums, but I'm not sure I can make it any harder—enums are a nice, elegant feature of the language, and really don't take much explaining—at least for basic usage.

What just happened?

I know there are many of you out there wondering about what goes on under the hood. Here are the highlights about how you can use enums, and their basic construction:

Enums are classes

As a result, you get type-safety, compile-time checking, and the ability to use them in variable declarations. This beats the proverbial pants off of integer constants (see the "What about..." section in this lab).

Enums extend java.lang.Enum

java.lang.Enum is a new class in Tiger, and is not itself an enumerated type. All enumerated types implicitly extend Enum.

"Grade" is the type; A, B, C, and so forth are the values for that type. Enum terminology is a bit confusing, so it's good to keep these straight.

Enumerated types aren't integers

Each declared value is an instance of the enum class itself; this ensures type-safety and allows for even more compile-time checking.

Enums have no public constructor

This removes the ability to create additional instances of the enum not defined at compile-time. Only those instances defined by the enum are available.

Enum values are public, static, and final

Values cannot be overwritten, changed, or otherwise messed with in ways that affect your programming logic. The enum itself is effectively final, as it cannot be subclassed (see "Extending an Enum"). In fact, the specification says that you are not allowed to declare an enum as final or abstract, as the compiler will take care of those details.

Enum values can be compared with == or equals( )

Because enums are effectively final, and there is a distinct set of values, you can use—for comparison. Additionally, enumerated types have a working equals( ), for use in collection classes (see "Maps of Enums" and "Sets of Enums" later in this chapter).

Enums are not "final" when they have value-specific methods, discussed later in the chapter.

Enums implements java.lang.Comparable

As a result, enum values can be compared with compareTo( ), and ordering occurs in the same order as values are declared in the enum declaration.

Enums override toString( )

The toString( ) method on an enumerated type returns the name of the value. Grade.INCOMPLETE.toString( ) returns the String "INCOMPLETE". However, this method isn't final, and can be overridden if desired.

Enums provide a valueOf( ) method

The static valueOf( ) method complements toString( ). Grade.valueOf("INCOMPLETE") returns Grade.INCOMPLETE.

WARNING

If you change the behavior of toString( ), you need to also change the behavior of valueOf( ). These two methods should always be mirror images of each other.

Enums define a final instance method named ordinal( )

> oridinal( ) returns the integer position of each enumerated value, starting at zero, based on the declaration order in the enum. This isn't a method you should use in your own code, but it's used by other enum-related functionality, so is worth knowing about.

Enums define a values( ) *method*

> values( ) allows for iteration over the values of an enum, as detailed later in this chapter in "Iterating Over Enums".

What about...

...doing this in Java 1.4 (and previous releases)? At first glance, you may not see all the advantages that enums offer, especially if you're comfortable with static and final variables (essentially constants) in pre-Tiger JDKs. In fact, the Grade class should look an awful lot like the OldGrade class shown in Example 3-3, which is how you might write Grade in a pre-Tiger environment.

Example 3-3. Writing enums in pre-Tiger JDKs

```
package com.oreilly.tiger.ch03;

public class OldGrade {
  public static final int A = 1;
  public static final int B = 2;
  public static final int C = 3;
  public static final int D = 4;
  public static final int F = 5;
  public static final int INCOMPLETE = 6;
}
```

However, there are a lot of problems that aren't immediately apparent. First, consider that the following line of code is legal if you are using OldGrade:

```
student1.assignGrade(1);
```

If you move to Tiger, though, and declare that assignGrade( ) only accepts a Grade enum, that same line will result in a compiler error:

```
[javac] code\src\ch03\GradeTester.java:19:
        assignGrade(com.oreilly.tiger.ch03.Grade) in
        com.oreilly.tiger.ch03.Student can not be applied to (int)
[javac]     student1.assignGrade(1);
```

Your error may look a little different—I formatted this to be readable on the page of a book.

Using the OldGrade class, you aren't passing in an object of a specific type; you're just passing in an int, that happens (in your specific program implementation) to be associated with the variable name OldGrade.A. You should see the enormous ability to misuse these integer constants, because they're not strongly typed to a specific grade.

Even worse, consider using this same system (Student and OldGrade), but with another "constant" class:

```
public class OldClass {
  public static final int EnglishLit      = 1;
  public static final int Calculus        = 2;
  public static final int MusicTheory     = 3;
  public static final int MusicPerformance = 4;
}
```

Now things get even hairier, because suddenly the following code is legal:

```
student1.assignGrade(OldClass.EnglishList);
```

Some junior programmer's typo suddenly gave this student an A! Enumerated types may seem like a minor convenience, but they turn out to be a major step forward for Java. Use them often, and let the compiler catch your mistakes, rather than a late-night debugging session.

Declaring Enums Inline

While it's useful to create a separate enum class, defined in its own source file, sometimes its also useful to just define an enum, use it, and throw it away. This is possible through member types.

How do I do that?

Just define the enum within your class, as you would any other member variable. You might need a DownloadStatus enum, for example, but only within a Downloader class:

```
public class Downloader {

  public enum DownloadStatus { INITIALIZING, IN_PROGRESS, COMPLETE };

  // Class body
}
```

Oddly enough, this same code may be written as follows:

```
public class Downloader {

  public static enum DownloadStatus { INITIALIZING, IN_PROGRESS, COMPLETE };

  // Class body
}
```

In this case, the static modifier has been added. This has no effective change on the enum, as nested enums are implicitly static. In other words, it's sort of like declaring an interface abstract—it's redundant. Because of this redundancy, I'd recommend *against* using the static keyword in these declarations.

Iterating Over Enums

Ever been given a class with lousy documentation, no source code, and little instruction on its use? Welcome to the loosely knit organization of real-world programmers. In many cases, you can resort to reflection to figure out what a class has to offer in lieu of source code, and of course JavaDoc is always helpful. In the case of enumerated types, though, there's a nice built-in feature: the values() method. This method provides access to all of the types within an enum.

Examples in the enum specification also omit "static" in nested declarations.

How do I do that?

Invoking the values() method on an enum returns an array of all the values in the type:

```
public void listGradeValues(PrintStream out) throws IOException {
  Grade[] gradeValues = Grade.values();
  for (Grade g : Grade.values()) {
    out.println("Allowed value: '" + g + "'");
  }
}
```

This is a nice way to get a quick dump of all the allowed values for a particular enum:

```
run-ch03:
    [echo] Running Chapter 3 examples from Java 1.5: A Developer's Notebook

    [echo] Running GradeTester...
    [java] Allowed value: 'A'
    [java] Allowed value: 'B'
    [java] Allowed value: 'C'
    [java] Allowed value: 'D'
    [java] Allowed value: 'F'
    [java] Allowed value: 'INCOMPLETE'
```

Run this sample with the Ant target "run-ch03".

What just happened?

First, note that type-safety is employed. values() doesn't return an array of String values—instead it returns an array of Grade instances. In the out.println() statement, each Grade has its toString() method executed, which in turn *does* provide a String name for the value. At no point are you working with integer constants or even String values—the Grade object hides all these implementation details from you, and allows strict compile-time checking.

What about...

...using a for/in loop? Well, you're ahead of me—for/in isn't covered until Chapter 7. Still, for those of you who are curious, you can indeed perform the same iteration with Tiger's new for/in capabilities:

```
// for/in loop
for (Grade g : grade.values()) {
  out.println("Allowed value: '" + g + "'");
}
```

Switching on Enums

As you begin to integrate enums into your own programs, one of the first tasks you'll want to accomplish is using an enum with a switch statement. This is a pretty obvious application; there's little value in using enums if you can't easily react to the set of values available.

How do I do that?

Prior to Java 1.4, switch only worked with int, short, char, and byte values. However, since enums have a finite set of values, Tiger adds switch support for them. Here's an example of using an enum in a switch statement:

This code assumes that student1 has already been created; this is taken care of in the test class, "GradeTester".

```
public void testSwitchStatement(PrintStream out) throws IOException {
    StringBuffer outputText = new StringBuffer(student1.getFullName());

    switch (student1.getGrade()) {
      case A:
        outputText.append(" excelled with a grade of A");
        break;
      case B: // fall through to C
      case C:
        outputText.append(" passed with a grade of ")
                  .append(student1.getGrade().toString());
        break;
      case D: // fall through to F
      case F:
        outputText.append(" failed with a grade of ")
                  .append(student1.getGrade().toString());
        break;
      case INCOMPLETE:
```

```
        outputText.append(" did not complete the class.");
        break;
    }

    out.println(outputText.toString());
}
```

The argument to switch must be an enumerated value; in this case, the return type of getGrade( ) is Grade, which meets these requirements. However, there is another requirement that makes this code a little odd-- did you catch it? Note the format of each case clause:

```
case A:
case B:
case C:
case D:
case F:
case INCOMPLETE:
```

See anything missing? How about the enum class identifier:

```
case Grade.A:
case Grade.B:
case Grade.C:
case Grade.D:
case Grade.F:
case Grade.INCOMPLETE:
```

For those of you up on Tiger, this may make you think about the import static feature of the language, which I cover in Chapter 8. However, the two have no relation (except perhaps on an implementation level)—Tiger simply *requires* that you not preface each enumerated type with the enum class name. In fact, it's a compilation error if you do! Sort of a nice convenience function, I think.

There's another issue you should be careful about—not handling every enumerated type. In the following version of the switch, I've left out handling of Grade.D:

```
switch (student1.getGrade()) {
  case A:
    outputText.append(" excelled with a grade of A");
    break;
  case B: // fall through to C
  case C:
    outputText.append(" passed with a grade of ")
            .append(student1.getGrade().toString());
    break;
  case F:
    outputText.append(" failed with a grade of ")
            .append(student1.getGrade().toString());
    break;
  case INCOMPLETE:
```

```
      outputText.append(" did not complete the class.");
      break;
  }
```

It's not completely clear as to if the compiler will be *required* to issue a warning if all types aren't handled; however, it is clear that this is bad coding. You need to be sure that every possible enumerated type is handled, or get ready for some late-night debugging sessions.

You can compile the book's code with warnings turned on with "ant check-compile". All "-Xlint" warnings will be displayed.

TIP

As of this writing, the Tiger compiler did *not* issue a -Xlint warning in this situation.

What just happened?

The handling of an enumerated type by the compiler is a little different than the handling of an integral type. That difference stems from enum values not being compile-time constants; in other words, your code is not turned into the following at compile-time:

```
switch (student1.getGrade()) {
    case 0:
       outputText.append(" excelled with a grade of A");
       break;
    case 1: // fall through to C
    case 2:
       outputText.append(" passed with a grade of ")
                 .append(student1.getGrade().toString());
       break;
    case 3: // fall through to F
    case 4:
       outputText.append(" failed with a grade of ")
                 .append(student1.getGrade().toString());
       break;
    case 5:
       outputText.append(" did not complete the class.");
       break;
  }
```

Instead, assuming that the enum and switch statement exist in the same compilation unit, a *jump table* is created, relating each enumerated type to the value of ordinal( ), invoked on each type. That results in nearly the same performance as the inlining shown above; the ordinal values aren't inserted into the code, but the compiler can look them up in the jump table extremely quickly. If the enum is changed and recompiled, the jump table is updated, and there's no problem.

More often than not, though, the switch and enum are *not* in the same compilation unit, and this is not possible. In these cases, most compilers turn the switch statement into a series of if/else statements:

```
Grade tmp = student1.getGrade();
if (tmp == Grade.A)
    outputText.append(" excelled with a grade of A");
else if ((tmp == Grade.B) || (tmp == Grade.C))
    outputText.append(" passed with a grade of ")
             .append(student1.getGrade().toString());
else if ((tmp == Grade.D) || (tmp == Grade.F))
    outputText.append(" failed with a grade of ")
              .append(student1.getGrade().toString());
else if (tmp == Grade.INCOMPLETE)
    outputText.append(" did not complete the class.");
```

This isn't efficient as a jump table, but this ensures that if the enum is changed in one compilation unit, the switch statement (in a different unit) continues to function properly. It also removes the need to worry about reordering of an enum, which would affect a jump table.

What about...

...using the default keyword? It's perfectly legal, and in fact strongly recommended. Since enum is a new type in Java, it would be easy for someone to come along and add a new type to your enum without you knowing about it:

```
public enum Grade { A, B, C, D, F, INCOMPLETE,
                    WITHDREW_PASSING, WITHDREW_FAILING };
```

Now, your switch code will fail because it doesn't account for all the possible Grade values. It's better to plan for this with a little more robust code:

```
switch (student1.getGrade()) {
  case A:
    outputText.append(" excelled with a grade of A");
    break;
  case B: // fall through to C
  case C:
    outputText.append(" passed with a grade of ")
              .append(student1.getGrade().toString());
    break;
  case D: // fall through to F
  case F:
    outputText.append(" failed with a grade of ")
              .append(student1.getGrade().toString());
    break;
  case INCOMPLETE:
    outputText.append(" did not complete the class.");
```

"default" is best used in this way, to catch unexpected values—it's generally good programming practice to specifically handle every known value, though, as that makes your code much clearer. "default" should be for handling unknown conditions, and not used as a catch-all.

```
        break;
    default:
        outputText.append(" has a grade of ")
                  .append(student1.getGrade().toString());
}
```

An even better idea would be to throw some sort of error on an unexpected type--this will ensure that you and other programmers realize that something is out of sync:

```
default: throw new AssertionError("Unexpected enumerated value!");
```

Maps of Enums

Once you've gotten your fingers used to typing public enum, you'll start to find all sorts of interesting uses for enums. Once you've gotten past the very basic constant-replacement, you'll start to see that they also serve as great keys, or indices, in collection-type structures. Apparently the Sun guys thought the same thing, and provided a nice facility for working with enums as indices.

How do I do that?

In the old, archaic, pre-Tiger days (snicker, snicker), you might have used a constants class like OldAntStatus (you'll remember a similar class from Example 3-3):

```
public class OldAntStatus {
    public static final int INITIALIZING = 0;
    public static final int COMPILING    = 1;
    public static final int COPYING      = 2;
    public static final int JARRING      = 3;
    public static final int ZIPPING      = 4;
    public static final int DONE         = 5;
    public static final int ERROR        = 6;
}
```

You might then write a simple array of messages that are associated with each of these status codes:

```
String[] antMessages = new String[] {
    "Initalizing Ant...",       // INITIALIZING
    "Compiling Java classes...", // COMPILING
    "Copying files...",         // COPYING
    "JARring up files...",      // JARRING
    "ZIPping up files...",      // ZIPPING
    "Build complete.",          // DONE
    "Error occurred."           // ERROR
}
```

You can then access the appropriate message using the constant:

```
    int antStatus = antProcess.getStatus();
    out.println("ant> " + antMessages[antStatus]);
```

It's a pretty valid desire to want to accomplish the same sorts of tasks with enumerated types, and get all the benefits of enums along the way. You'll need to use the java.util.EnumMap class to accomplish this, which is a new collection type just perfect for the job. First, you need to define the enum you want to use for a keyset, as shown in Example 3-4.

Example 3-4. An enum to use for a keyset

```
package com.oreilly.tiger.ch03;

public enum AntStatus {
  INITIALIZING,
  COMPILING,
  COPYING,
  JARRING,
  ZIPPING,
  DONE,
  ERROR
}
```

You can now create a new EnumMap, in conjunction with generics—declare the enumerated type you want to use for the key, and the class type you want to use for the value:

```
EnumMap<AntStatus, String> antMessages;
```

Then, when creating a new instance, you pass the EnumMap the Class object for the enum used for the keyset:

```
EnumMap<AntStatus, String> antMessages =
  EnumMap<AntStatus, String>(AntStatus.class);
```

Remember to declare the types being used, key and value, in both the variable declaration and the variable instantiation.

TIP

This should further emphasize the fact that enums are really just Java classes that the compiler handles specially. This is discussed in more detail in the "Creating an Enum" lab.

Once the initialization is taken care of, things get very simple. You just seed the values, and use them:

```
public void testEnumMap(PrintStream out) throws IOException {
  // Create a map with the key and a String message
  EnumMap<AntStatus, String> antMessages =
    new EnumMap<AntStatus, String>(AntStatus.class);

  // Initialize the map
  antMessages.put(AntStatus.INITIALIZING, "Initializing Ant...");
```

This code is in AntStatusTester.java.

```
antMessages.put(AntStatus.COMPILING,    "Compiling Java classes...");
antMessages.put(AntStatus.COPYING,      "Copying files...");
antMessages.put(AntStatus.JARRING,      "JARring up files...");
antMessages.put(AntStatus.ZIPPING,      "ZIPping up files...");
antMessages.put(AntStatus.DONE,         "Build complete.");
antMessages.put(AntStatus.ERROR,        "Error occurred.");

// Iterate and print messages
for (AntStatus status : AntStatus.values() ) {
  out.println("For status " + status + ", message is: " +
            antMessages.get(status));
}
}
```

Running this code nicely prints out all the status codes, and the associated message with each:

```
[echo] Running AntStatusTester...
[java] For status INITIALIZING, message is: Initializing Ant...
[java] For status COMPILING, message is: Compiling Java classes...
[java] For status COPYING, message is: Copying files...
[java] For status JARRING, message is: JARring up files...
[java] For status ZIPPING, message is: ZIPping up files...
[java] For status DONE, message is: Build complete.
[java] For status ERROR, message is: Error occurred.
```

Of course, as an added benefit, EnumMap protects you from mis-ordering when initializing values, reordering in the enumerated type, and just about any other strange situation that can arise from more than one person working on code at the same time.

Sets of Enums

Another common usage of constants is to represent a feature set of a particular item, such as a car, or even something really exciting, like a guitar. You could then use bitwise operators to compare or check for specific features. As in the lab on "Maps of Enums," the Java language folks realized this, and added another collection class for the purpose, java.util. EnumSet.

How do I do that?

First, examine the way this scenario might be handled in pre-Tiger days. Example 3-5 is a simple class that defines some common guitar features.

Example 3-5. Guitar feature set

```
package com.oreilly.tiger.ch03;

public class OldGuitarFeatures {
```

Example 3-5. Guitar feature set (continued)

```
    public static final int ROSEWOOD     = 0x01; // back/sides
    public static final int MAHOGANY     = 0x02; // back/sides
    public static final int ZIRICOTE     = 0x04; // back/sides

    public static final int SPRUCE       = 0x10; // top
    public static final int CEDAR        = 0x12; // top

    public static final int AB_ROSETTE   = 0x30; // abalone rosette
    public static final int AB_TOP_BORDER = 0x32; // abalone top border

    public static final int IL_DIAMONDS  = 0x40; // diamond/square inlay
    public static final int IL_DOTS      = 0x42; // dots inlays

}
```

These are all features, and are all represented by powers of two. That allows them to be combined like this:

```
int bourgeoisD150 = OldGuitarFeatures.ROSEWOOD |
                    OldGuitarFeatures.SPRUCE |
                    OldGuitarFeatures.AB_ROSETTE |
                    OldGuitarFeatures.IL_DIAMONDS;
```

With this initial work done (you could represent every guitar in a line this way), you can test a specific guitar for a specific features, using the bitwise AND operator:

```
boolean hasAbRosette = (bourgeoisD150 & OldGuitarFeatures.IL_DIAMONDS) != 0;
```

Looking at the constants in OldGuitarFeatures, you should see that they are just another case of an enumerated type, and could be represented in Tiger as shown in Example 3-6.

Example 3-6. Representing guitar features in Tiger

```
package com.oreilly.tiger.ch03;

public enum GuitarFeatures {
  ROSEWOOD, // back/sides
  MAHOGANY, // back/sides
  ZIRICOTE, // back/sides

  SPRUCE, // top
  CEDAR,  // top

  AB_ROSETTE,    // abalone rosette
  AB_TOP_BORDER, // abalone top border

  IL_DIAMONDS, // diamond/square inlay
  IL_DOTS      // dots inlays
}
```

Be sure and continue to compile with the "-source 1.5" switch. Using the provided Ant scripts takes care of this, by the way.

However, operating on these constants with bitwise operators isn't possible, at least without the help of a new class, java.util.EnumSet. Here are the methods of this class you should be concerned with, most of which are factories:

```
// Returns a new EnumSet with all elements from the supplied type
public static EnumSet allOf(Class elementType);

// Returns a new EnumSet of the same type as the supplied set, but
//    with all the values not in the supplied set; a mirror image
public static EnumSet complementOf(EnumSet e);

// Returns a new EnumSet from the provided collection
public static EnumSet copyOf(Collection c);

// Returns a new EnumSet with no values in it
public static EnumSet noneOf(Class elementType);

// Various methods to create an EnumSet with the supplied elements in it
public static EnumSet of(E e[, E e2, E e3, E e4, E e5]);

//Varags version
public static EnumSet of(E... e);

// Creates an EnumSet with a range of values
public static EnumSet range(E from, E to);

// returns a copy of the current set - not a factory method
public EnumSet clone();
```

You may have to look at this for a minute to get the sense of things—the format is rather odd. But, to create a new EnumSet of all guitar features, just use the following:

```
EnumSet allFeatures = EnumSet.allOf(GuitarFeatures);
```

Simple enough, right? If you want only the back and side woods, you could use this notation:

```
EnumSet backSides = EnumSet.of(GuitarFeatures.ROSEWOOD,
                               GuitarFeatures.MAHOGANY,
                               GuitarFeatures.ZIRICOTE);
```

You could also use the range( ) operator:

```
EnumSet backSides = EnumSet.range(GuitarFeatures.ROSEWOOD,
                                  GuitarFeatures.ZIRICOTE);
```

WARNING

This is really a bad idea—reordering of the enum screws this up, and you can never really completely insulate yourself from that possibility. Always use of( ) instead of range( ), if at all possible.

---

complentOf( ) is also a handy method:

```
EnumSet noAbalone = EnumSet.complementOf(
        EnumSet.of(GuitarFeatures.AB_ROSETTE, GuitarFeatures.AB_TOP_BORDER));
```

With your setup done, you can just use the contains( ) method, available to all collection classes, to check for a value or values:

```
EnumSet bourgeoisD150 = EnumSet.of(GuitarFeatures.ROSEWOOD,
                                   GuitarFeatures.SPRUCE,
                                   GuitarFeatures.AB_ROSETTE,
                                   GuitarFeatures.IL_DIAMONDS);

boolean hasAbRosette = bourgeoisD150.contains(GuitarFeatures.AB_ROSETTE);
```

- You can't use varargs to work with the of( ) method, due to the usage of generic types in the factory method. Variable arguments are detailed in Chapter 5.

Adding Methods to an Enum

Those of you paying attention should have noticed something pretty important that I said earlier in this chapter in the "Creating an Enum" lab—that enums are just Java classes. They have some special behavior that you get for free, but ultimately they are indeed compiled classes. What's important about this is that it implies that you can do some pretty cool things with enums beyond the basics you've seen so far—such as adding methods to the enum. This is a great way to make your enum even more valuable to application programmers.

How do I do that?

Adding methods to an enum works just like adding methods to a normal Java class. Example 3-7 is a beefed-up version of GuitarFeatures that adds several new methods.

Example 3-7. Adding methods to an enum

```
package com.oreilly.tiger.ch03;

public enum GuitarFeatures {

  ROSEWOOD(0),        // back/sides
  MAHOGANY(0),        // back/sides
  ZIRICOTE(300),      // back/sides

  SPRUCE(0),          // top
  CEDAR(0),           // top

  AB_ROSETTE(75),     // abalone rosette
  AB_TOP_BORDER(400), // abalone top border

  IL_DIAMONDS(150),   // diamond/square inlay
```

Example 3-7. Adding methods to an enum (continued)

```
IL_DOTS(0);           // dots inlays

/** The upcharge for the feature */
private float upcharge;

GuitarFeatures(float upcharge) {
  this.upcharge = upcharge;
}

public float getUpcharge() {
  return upcharge;
}
}

public String getDescription() {
  switch(this) {
    case ROSEWOOD:      return "Rosewood back and sides";
    case MAHOGANY:      return "Mahogany back and sides";
    case ZIRICOTE:      return "Ziricote back and sides";
    case SPRUCE:        return "Sitka Spruce top";
    case CEDAR:         return "Wester Red Cedar top";
    case AB_ROSETTE:    return "Abalone rosette";
    case AB_TOP_BORDER: return "Abalone top border";
    case IL_DIAMONDS:
      return "Diamonds and squares fretboard inlay";
    case IL_DOTS:
      return "Small dots fretboard inlay";
    default: return "Unknown feature";
  }
}
}
```

There are quite a few things here that you'll need to take note of. First, the class now has a constructor that takes in a `float` parameter for the upcharge of each feature. As a result, each enumerated type now passes in a parameter to the constructor:

```
ROSEWOOD(0),        // back/sides
MAHOGANY(0),        // back/sides
ZIRICOTE(300),      // back/sides

SPRUCE(0),          // top
CEDAR(0),           // top

AB_ROSETTE(75),     // abalone rosette
AB_TOP_BORDER(400), // abalone top border

IL_DIAMONDS(150),   // diamond/square inlay
IL_DOTS(0);         // dots inlays
```

This looks a little odd in the code, but opens up a world of possibilities for information to be passed in for each value. You should also notice that the final value is followed by a semicolon. This denotes the end of the values section, and is required.

Then, variables are declared, and methods appear, just like any other class. In the example, getUpcharge( ) returns the value supplied to the constructor, and getDescription( ) supplies a human-readable version of the feature. You'll see that switch is used, as described in "Switching on Enums," and this makes the method body simple to read and understand.

WARNING

You cannot put your variable declarations before the enumerated values. The following code, for example, won't compile:

```
public enum GuitarFeatures {
  private float upcharge;

  ROSEWOOD,
  MAHOGANY,      // etc.
}
```

All declarations must follow the enumerated type declarations.

What about...

...limiting access to the enum constructor? Enum constructors are implicitly private, so this is taken care of for you. In some programming techniques, such as singletons, access modifiers are placed in front of the constructor so that it can't be directly accessed:

```
public enum GuitarFeatures {

  ROSEWOOD(0),          // back/sides
  MAHOGANY(0),          // back/sides
  ZIRICOTE(300),        // back/sides

  SPRUCE(0),            // top
  CEDAR(0),             // top

  AB_ROSETTE(75),       // abalone rosette
  AB_TOP_BORDER(400),   // abalone top border

  IL_DIAMONDS(150),     // diamond/square inlay
  IL_DOTS(0);           // dots inlays
```

```
/** The upcharge for the feature */
private float upcharge;

private GuitarFeatures(float upcharge) {
  this.upcharge = upcharge;
}

// Other method bodies

}
```

This compiles, but it just explicitly does what the compiler takes care of for you—making the constructor private. However, you *cannot* supply the standard public modifier:

```
public GuitarFeatures(float upcharge) {
  this.upcharge = upcharge;
}
```

If you try this, you'll get a compiler error:

```
[javac] src\ch03\GuitarFeatures.java:21:
        modifier public not allowed here
[javac]    public GuitarFeatures(float upcharge) {
[javac]           ^
```

So leave *all* modifiers off of enum constructors.

Implementing Interfaces with Enums

Now that you're starting to add methods to your enums (see the previous lab on "Adding Methods to an Enum" for details if you're skipping around), you may find that you want to define methods in an interface, and implement that interface with one, two, or even more enums. You may also want to have an enum implement an interface, and have classes implement that same interface. All this is possible, and even quite simple.

How do I do that?

Example 3-8 is a very simple interface that could describe enumerated types that represent features on all sorts of instruments (not just guitars).

Example 3-8. Base interface for feature enums

```
package com.oreilly.tiger.ch03;

public interface Features {
```

Example 3-8. *Base interface for feature enums (continued)*

```
/** Get the upcharge for this feature */
public float getUpcharge();

/** Get the description for this feature */
public String getDescription();

}
```

It's trivial to make GuitarFeatures implement this interface, as the methods are already written:

```
public enum GuitarFeatures implements Features {
```

Now you can create BanjoFeatures, MandolinFeatures, and more, all using the same interface as a starting point. This creates a nice sense of uniformity among your enums, and is highly recommended.

Value-Specific Class Bodies

In covering the more advanced features of enums, I can't leave out the ability to define *value-specific class bodies*. That sounds sort of fancy, but all it means is that each enumerated value within a type can define value-specific methods. This is a rather obscure bit of functionality, but sort of cool to talk about around the water cooler.

How do I do that?

Example 3-9 is an example of a class that determines how the perform() method is executed based on the enumerated value. It's a perfect example of value-specific class bodies.

Example 3-9. *Value-specific class bodies in an enum*

This example is lifted straight out of Java in a Nutshell, Fifth Edition (O'Reilly).

```
// These are the opcodes that our stack machine can execute.
enum Opcode {

  // Push the single operand onto the stack
  PUSH(1) {
    public void perform(StackMachine machine, int[] operands) {
      machine.push(operands[0]);
    }
  }, // Remember to separate enum values with commas

  // Add the top two values on the stack and put the result
  ADD(0) {
    public void perform(StackMachine machine, int[] operands) {
```

Example 3-9. Value-specific class bodies in an enum (continued)

```
        machine.push(machine.pop() + machine.pop());
      }
   },

/* Other opcode values have been omitted for brevity */

   // Branch if Equal to Zero
   BEZ(1) {
     public void perform(StackMachine machine, int[] operands) {
       if (machine.pop() == 0) machine.setPC(operands[0]);
     }
   }; // Remember the required semicolon after last enum value

   // This is the constructor for the type.
   Opcode(int numOperands) { this.numOperands = numOperands; }

   int numOperands; // how many integer operands does it expect?

   // Each opcode constant must implement this abstract method in a
   // value-specific class body to perform the operation it represents.
   public abstract void perform(StackMachine machine, int[] operands);
}
```

Skipping past the individual types (which you should already understand), the method that each value should implement is defined: perform( ), which takes two arguments. Finally, each value is followed by an opening curly brace, one or more value-specific methods, and then a closing curly brace. This works in conjunction with any constructor that must be supplied a value, as this enum has. The end result, frankly, is one of the oddest looking Java constructs you'll ever see.

What just happened?

In the lab on "Creating an Enum," I mentioned that enumerated type values are created and marked as final (in addition to being public and static), ensuring that they aren't changed by some malicious or unknowing programmer. In the case of a value-specific class body, though, this isn't possible. Instead, an anonymous subclass of the type is created, and the value becomes a singleton instance of that subclass. This still ensures that multiple instances of the same value aren't floating around, but it does change what's going on at the compiler level a bit. Despite this, you still can't extend an enum (see "Extending an Enum" for more details).

I suppose you could really clutter things up with generics and varargs, but you get the idea... value-specific class bodies are often a pain to debug for even mid-level programmers, because of their unusual syntax.

What about...

...just using a more generic method that determines what to do based on a switch statement? Well, that's a better idea, to be honest. Here's the (much cleaner) way to write OpCode:

```
// These are the the opcodes that our stack machine can execute.
abstract static enum Opcode {
  PUSH(1),
  ADD(0),
  BEZ(1); // Remember the required semicolon after last enum value

  int numOperands;

  Opcode(int numOperands) { this.numOperands = numOperands; }

  public void perform(StackMachine machine, int[] operands) {
    switch(this) {
      case PUSH: machine.push(operands[0]); break;
      case ADD: machine.push(machine.pop() + machine.pop()); break;
      case BEZ: if (machine.pop() == 0) machine.setPC(operands[0]); break;
      default: throw new AssertionError();
    }
  }
}
```

This is so painfully simpler than the first version of OpCode that I hesitated to even include this lab—but for completeness, here it is. If at all possible, though, consider using switch in your method bodies to direct program flow, rather than value-specific class bodies.

Manually Defining an Enum

You'll recall from the first lab, "Creating an Enum," that all enums implicitly extend the new java.lang.Enum class. This class looks a bit like Example 3-10; I've trimmed the method implementations and just left the declarations in for clarity.

Example 3-10. The java.lang.Enum class

```
package java.lang;

public class Enum<E extends Enum<E>> implements Comparable<E>, Serializable {

  protected Enum(String name, int ordinal);

  protected Object clone();
  public int compareTo(E o);
  public boolean equals(Object other);
```

This code listing is extracted from the Java 1.5 JavaDoc. Source code isn't available as of the time of this writing.

Example 3-10. The java.lang.Enum class (continued)

```
    public Class<E> getDeclaringClass();
    public int hashCode();
    public String name();
    public int ordinal();
    public String toString();
    public static <T extends Enum<T>> T valueOf(Class<T> enumType, String name);
}
```

If you're a bit of a hack, that may get your mind wandering...couldn't I just manually define my own enum, then? Good question.

How do I do that?

You don't—at least, not in Tiger. While this is very much an accessible class, and is indeed the base class of all enumerated types in Tiger, the compiler won't let you extend it, as Example 3-11 tries to do.

Example 3-11. Attempting to extend java.lang.Enum

```
package com.oreilly.tiger.ch03;

public class ExtendedEnum extends Enum {
}
```

Attempting to compile this class give you the following error:

```
[javac] src\ch03\ExtendedEnum.java:3:
            classes cannot directly extend java.lang.Enum
[javac] public class ExtendedEnum extends Enum {
[javac]                ^
```

Extending an Enum

It's often easy to define a hierarchy of enumerations. In this scenario, one enum represents a base type of allowed values. Subclasses of that enum would add additional values to the base enum, perhaps specialized to a certain task.

How do I do that?

Here's another one of those pesky, "You don't" labs. Tiger does not allow extension of an enum. For example, consider Example 3-12, a simple extension of the Grade enum defined back in Example 3-1.

Example 3-12. Extending the Grade enum

```
package com.oreilly.tiger.ch03;

public enum CollegeGrade extends Grade { DROP_PASSING, DROP_FAILING }
```

In theory, this would take the values Grade.A, Grade.B, and so forth, and add to them two new values, CollegeGrade.DROP_PASSING and CollegeGrade.DROP_FAILING. However, you'll get compilation errors if you try this:

```
compile-ch03-errors:
     [echo] Compiling all Java files...
    [javac] Compiling 13 source files to classes
    [javac] src\ch03\CollegeGrade.java:3: '{' expected
    [javac] public enum CollegeGrade extends Grade {DROP_PASSING, DROP_
FAILING}
    [javac]                                  ^
    [javac] src\ch03\CollegeGrade.java:3: <identifier> expected
    [javac] public enum CollegeGrade extends Grade {DROP_PASSING, DROP_
FAILING}
    [javac]
  ^
    [javac] 2 errors
```

What about...

...using a class to extend an enum, instead of another enum? That doesn't work either. There's just no getting around this limitation, at least that I've been able to find..

Use the Ant target "compile-ch03-errors" to try and compile the CollegeGrade.java source file.

If you find a sneaky way to extend an enum, let us know! We'll add it to the next edition.

Autoboxing and Unboxing

When you begin to study Java, one of the first lessons is always about objects. In fact, you could say that java.lang.Object is the very corner-stone of Java. Practically 99% of everything you do in the language revolves around that class, or one of its subclasses. It's the 1% of the time, though, that can be a pain—when you suddenly find yourself having to convert between your objects and Java primitives.

Primitives in Java are your ints, shorts, chars, and so on—types that aren't objects at all. As a result, Java has *wrapper classes*, such as Integer, Short, and Character, which are object versions of the primitive types. Where things get annoying is when you have to go back and forth between the two—converting a primitive to its wrapper, using it, then converting the object's value back to a primitive. Suddenly, methods such as intValue( ) begin to litter your code.

Happily, Tiger finally takes care of this issue, at least as much as can be expected without tossing out primitives completely. This is handled through two new conversion features: boxing and unboxing. And, just to add some more words to the English language, it does these conversions automatically, so we now talk about autoboxing and auto-unboxing.

Converting Primitives to Wrapper Types

Literal values in Java are always primitives. The number 0, for example, is an int, and must be converted to an object through code like this:

```
Integer i = new Integer(0);
```

This is pretty silly, for obvious reasons, and Tiger removes the need for such nonsense through boxing.

How do I do that?

You can now dispense with the manual conversions, and let the Java virtual machine (VM) handle conversion of primitives to object wrapper types:

```
Integer i = 0;
```

In the background, Java handles taking this primitive and turning it into a wrapper type. The same conversion happens with explicit primitive types:

```
int foo = 0;
Integer integer = foo;
```

If you're not completely convinced of the value of this, try typing these statements into a pre-Tiger compiler, and watch in amazement as you get some rather ridiculous errors:

```
compile-1.4:
     [echo] Compiling all Java files...
    [javac] Compiling 1 source file to classes
    [javac] src\com\oreilly\tiger\ch04\ConversionTester.java:6: incompatible
types
    [javac] found    : int
    [javac] required: java.lang.Integer
    [javac]      Integer i = 0;
    [javac]                ^
    [javac] src\com\oreilly\tiger\ch04\ConversionTester.java:9: incompatible
types
    [javac] found    : int
    [javac] required: java.lang.Integer
    [javac]      Integer integer = foo;
    [javac]                      ^
    [javac] 2 errors
```

The "compile-1.4" target compiles the examples from this chapter with the "-source 1.4" switch.

These errors "magically" disappear in Tiger when using the source 1.5 switch.

What just happened?

Behind the scenes, these primitive values are *boxed*. Boxing refers to the conversion from a primitive to its corresponding wrapper type: `Boolean`, `Byte`, `Short`, `Character`, `Integer`, `Long`, `Float`, or `Double`. Because this happens automatically, it's generally referred to as *autoboxing*.

It's also common for Java to perform a widening conversion in addition to boxing a value:

```
Number n = 0.0f;
```

Here, the literal is boxed into a `Float`, and then widened into a `Number`.

Additionally, the Java specification indicates that certain primitives are always to be boxed into the same immutable wrapper objects. These objects are then cached and reused, with the expectation that these are commonly used objects. These special values are the boolean values true and false, all byte values, short and int values between –128 and 127, and any char in the range \u0000 to \u007F. As this all happens behind the scenes, it's more of an implementation detail than something you need to worry much about.

Converting Wrapper Types to Primitives

Just as Tiger converts primitives to wrapper types as needed, the reverse is also true. Like boxing, *unboxing* involves little effort on the part of the programmer.

How do I do that?

Here's some more simple code that does both boxing and unboxing, all without any special instruction:

```
// Boxing
int foo = 0;
Integer integer = foo;

// Simple Unboxing
int bar = integer;

Integer counter = 1;        // boxing
int counter2 = counter;     // unboxing
```

Pretty simple, isn't it?

What about...

...null value assignment? Since null is a legal value for an object, and therefore any wrapper type, the following code is legal:

```
Integer i = null;
int j = i;
```

i is assigned null (which is legal), and then i is unboxed into j. However, null isn't a legal value for a primitive, so this code throws a NullPointerException.

Incrementing and Decrementing Wrapper Types

When you begin to think about the implications of boxing and unboxing, you'll realize that they are far-reaching. Suddenly, every operation available to a primitive should be available to its wrapper-type counterpart, and vice versa. One of the immediate applications is the increment and decrement operations: ++ and --. Both of these operations now work for wrapper types.

How do I do that?

Well, without much work, actually:

```
Integer counter = 1;
while (true) {
  System.out.printf("Iteration %d%n", counter++);
  if (counter > 1000) break;
}
```

The variable `counter` is treated just as an `int` in this code.

What just happened?

It's worth noting that more happened here than perhaps meets the eye. Take this simple portion of the example code:

```
counter++
```

Remember that `counter` is an `Integer`. So the value in `counter` was first auto-unboxed into an `int`, as that's the type required for the ++ operator.

TIP

This is actually an important point—the ++ operator has *not* been changed to work with object wrapper types—it's only through autounboxing that this code works.

Once the value is unboxed, it is incremented. Then, the new value has to be stored back in `counter`, which requires a boxing operation. All this in a fraction of a second!

You might also notice that the `Integer` value of `counter` was compared to the literal, and therefore primitive, value 1000. This is just another example of autounboxing at work.

Boolean Versus boolean

The boolean type is a little bit of a special case for Java primitives, mostly because it has several logical operators associated with it, such as ! (not), || (or), and && (and). With unboxing, these are now useful for Boolean values as well.

How do I do that?

Any time you have an expression that uses !, ||, or &&, any Boolean values are unboxed to boolean primitive values, and evaluated accordingly:

```
Boolean case1 = true;
Boolean case2 = true;
boolean case3 = false;

Boolean result = (case1 || case2) && case3;
```

In this case, the result of the expression, a boolean, is boxed into the result variable.

What about...

...direct object comparison? Object comparison works as it always has:

```
Integer i1 = 256;
Integer i2 = 256;

if (i1 == i2) System.out.println("Equal!");
else System.out.println("Not equal!");
```

The result of running this code, at least in my JVM, is the text "Not equal!" In this case, there is *not* an unboxing operation involved. The literal 256 is boxed into two different Integer objects (again, in my JVM), and then those *objects* are compared with ==. The result is *false*, as the two objects are different instances, with different memory addresses. Because both sides of the == expression contain objects, no unboxing occurs.

For inquiring minds, primitives are boxed up to wrapper types in equality comparisons. For operators such as <, >=, and so forth, the wrapper types are unboxed to primitive types.

WARNING

You can't depend on this result; it's merely used as an illustration. Some JVMs may choose to try and optimize this code, and create one instance for both Integer objects, and in that case, the == operator would return a true result.

But, watch out! Remember (from "Converting Primitives to Wrapper Types"), that certain primitive values are unboxed into constant, immutable wrapper objects. So, the result of running the following code might be surprising to you:

```
Integer i1 = 100;
Integer i2 = 100;

if (i1 == i2) System.out.println("Equal!");
else System.out.println("Not equal!");
```

Here, you would get the text "Equal!" Remember that int values from -127 to 127 are in that range of immutable wrapper types, so the VM actually uses the same object instance (and therefore memory address) for both i1 and i2. As a result, == returns a true result. You have to watch out for this, as it can result in some very tricky, hard-to-find bugs.

Conditionals and Unboxing

One of the odder features of Java is the conditional operator, often called the *ternary operator*. This is the operator version of an if/else statement, represented by the ? character. Since it evaluates an expression, the unboxing features of Tiger affect it, too. You can use it with all sorts of new types.

How do I do that?

Here is the format of this operator:

```
[conditional expression] ? [expression1] : [expression2]
```

If [conditional expression] evaluates to true, then [expression1] is executed; otherwise [expression2] is. In pre-Tiger Java, [conditional expression] had to result in a boolean value. This was a bit of a pain if you had a method that returned a Boolean wrapper type, or an expression that involved a Boolean. In Tiger, this is no longer a problem, and the ternary operator happily gobbles up any unboxed Boolean values:

```
Boolean arriving = false;
Boolean late = true;

System.out.println(arriving ? (late ? "It's about time!" : "Hello!") :
                             (late ? "Better hurry!" : "Goodbye"));
```

What just happened?

The ternary operator is a little tricky, in both Java 1.4 and Tiger, so it's worth mentioning some additional details. In pre-Tiger environments, *[expression1]* and *[expression2]* had to either be of the same type, or one had to be assignable to the other. So both had to be String values, or one could be an int and the other a float (as an int could be widened to a float). In Tiger, the restrictions loosen a bit due to unboxing. One or both expressions can be unboxed, so one could be an Integer and the other could be a Float, for example. However, *both* will be unboxed, and the int will be widened to float, so the return type of the expression would be a float–the result is *not* boxed back into a Float.

Another addition to Tiger is automatic casting of reference to their intersection type. That's a mouthful, so here's an example:

Thanks to Java in a Nutshell, Fifth Edition (O'Reilly) for this example.

```
String s = "hello";
StringBuffer sb = new StringBuffer("world");
boolean mutable = true;

CharSequence cs = mutable ? sb : s;
```

In pre-Tiger environments, this would generate an error, as sb (a StringBuffer) and s (a String) cannot be assigned to each other. However, this code should really work, as both String and StringBuffer implement the CharSequence interface. However, you have to perform some casting:

```
CharSequence cs = mutable ? (CharSequence)sb : (CharSequence)s;
```

Technically, this is a feature of the generic support in Tiger, but it seemed appropriate to mention it here. Generics are covered in detail in Chapter 7.

In Tiger, though, any valid *intersection* of the two operands can be used. This is essentially any object, walking up the inheritance chain, that is common to both operands. In this case, CharSequence fits that criteria, and so is a valid return type.

As a side effect of this, note that two reference types (objects) *always* share java.lang.Object as a common ancestor, so any result of a ternary operation involving non-primitive operands can be assigned to java.lang.Object.

Control Statements and Unboxing

There are several control statements in Java that take as an argument a boolean value, or an expression that results to a boolean value. It shouldn't be much of a surprise that these expressions now also take

Boolean values. Additionally, the switch statement has an array of new types it will accept.

How do I do that?

if/else, while, and do all are affected by Tiger's ability to unbox Boolean values to boolean values. By now, this shouldn't require much explanation:

```
Boolean arriving = false;
Boolean late = true;

Integer peopleInRoom = 0;
int maxCapacity = 100;
boolean timeToLeave = false;
while (peopleInRoom < maxCapacity) {
  if (arriving) {
    System.out.println("It's good to see you.");
    peopleInRoom++;
  } else {
    peopleInRoom--;
  }
  if (timeToLeave) {
    do {
      System.out.printf("Hey, person %d, get out!%n", peopleInRoom);
      peopleInRoom--;
    } while (peopleInRoom > 0);
  }
}
```

You might want to be cautious running this code—it's actually an infinite loop.

There are several boxing and unboxing operations going on here, in several control statements. Browse through this code, and work mentally through each operation.

Another statement that benefits from unboxing is switch. In pre-Tiger JVMs, the switch statement accepts int, short, char, or byte values. With unboxing in play, you can now supply it with Integer, Short, Char, and Byte values as well, in addition to the introduction of enums.

Enums are covered in Chapter 3.

Method Overload Resolution

Boxing and unboxing offer a lot of solutions to common problems (or, at least annoyances) in Java programming. However, these solutions manage to introduce a few quirks of their own, particularly in the area of *method resolution*. Method resolution is the process by which the Java compiler determines which method is being invoked. You'll need to be careful, as unboxing and boxing affect this process.

How do I do that?

In the normal case, Java handles method resolution by using the name of the method. In cases where a method is overloaded, though, an extra step must be taken. The arguments to the method are examined, and matched up with the arguments that a specific version of the requested method accepts. If no matching argument list is found, you get a compiler error. Sounds simple enough, right? Well, consider the following two methods:

```java
public void doSomething(double num);

public void doSomething(Integer num);
```

Now supposed that you invoked doSomething( ):

```java
int foo = 1;
doSomething(foo);
```

Which method is called? In a pre-Tiger environment, this is easy to determine. The int is widened to a double, and doSomething(double num) is called. However, in a Tiger environment, it would seem that boxing would occur, and doSomething(Integer num) would be what the method invocation would resolve to. While that's reasonable, it is *not* what happens.

Imagine writing a program like this, compiling and testing it in Java 1.4, and then recompiling it under Tiger. Suddenly, things start going haywire! Obviously, this isn't acceptable. For that reason, method resolution in Tiger will *always* select the same method that would have been selected in Java 1.4. As a rule, you really shouldn't mess around with this sort of overloading anyway, if at all possible. Be as specific as possible in your method naming and argument lists, and this issue goes away.

What just happened?

In Tiger, because of these restrictions, method resolution is a three-pass process:

Varargs are detailed in Chapter 5.

1. The compiler attempts to locate the correct method without any boxing, unboxing, or vararg invocations. This will find any method that would have been invoked under Java 1.4 rules.

2. If the first pass fails, the compiler tries method resolution again, this time allowing boxing and unboxing conversions. Methods with varargs are *not* considered in this pass.

Chapter 4: Autoboxing and Unboxing

3. If the second pass fails, the compiler tries method resolution one last time, allowing boxing and unboxing, and also considers vararg methods.

These rules ensure that consistency with pre-Tiger environments is maintained.

CHAPTER 5

varargs

One of the coolest features of Java, and of any object-oriented language, is method overloading. While many might think Java's strengths are its typing, or all the fringe APIs it comes with, there's just something nice about having the same method name with a variety of acceptable arguments:

```
Guitar guitar = new Guitar("Bourgeois", "Country Boy Deluxe",
                GuitarWood.MAHOGANY, GuitarWood.ADIRONDACK,
                1.718);

Guitar guitar = new Guitar("Martin", "HD-28");

Guitar guitar = new Guitar("Collings", "CW-28"
                GuitarWood.BRAZILIAN_ROSEWOOD, GuitarWood.ADIRONDACK,
                1.718,
                GuitarInlay.NO_INLAY, GuitarInlay.NO_INLAY);
```

This code calls three versions of the constructor of a (fictional) Guitar class, meaning that information can be supplied when it's available, rather than forcing a user to know everything about their guitar at one time (many professionals couldn't tell you their guitar's width at the nut). Here are the constructors used:

```
public Guitar(String builder, String model) {
}

public Guitar(String builder, String model,
              GuitarWood backSidesWood, GuitarWood topWood,
              float nutWidth) {
}

public Guitar(String builder, String model,
              GuitarWood backSidesWood, GuitarWood topWood,
              float nutWidth,
              GuitarInlay fretboardInlay, GuitarInlay topInlay) {
}
```

However, things start to get a little less useful when you want to add information that isn't finite. For example, suppose you want to allow additional, unspecified features to be added to this constructor. Here are some possible invocation examples:

```
Guitar guitar = new Guitar("Collings", "CW-28"
                    GuitarWood.BRAZILIAN_ROSEWOOD, GuitarWood.ADIRONDACK,
                    1.718,
                    GuitarInlay.NO_INLAY, GuitarInlay.NO_INLAY,
                    "Enlarged Soundhole", "No Popsicle Brace");

Guitar guitar = new Guitar("Martin", "HD-28V",
                    "Hot-rodded by Dan Lashbrook", "Fossil Ivory Nut",
                    "Fossil Ivory Saddle", "Low-profile bridge pins");
```

For these two cases alone, you'd have to add another constructor that takes two additional strings, and yet another that takes four additional strings. Try and apply these same versions to the already-overloaded constructor, and you'd end up with 20 or 30 versions of that silly constructor!

It's here where *variable arguments*, more often called *varargs*, come in. Another of Tiger's additions, varargs solve the problem detailed here once and for all, in a pretty slick way. This chapter covers this relatively simple feature in all its glory, and will have you writing better, cleaner, more flexible code in no time.

All of the new formatting methods, which are detailed in Chapter 9, use varargs.

Creating a Variable-Length Argument List

Variable arguments allow you to specify that a method can take multiple arguments of the same type, and don't require that the number of arguments be pre-determined (at compile- or runtime). This is one of the integral parts of Tiger, in fact, as several of the new features of the language actually incorporate varargs..

How do I do that?

First, get used to typing the ellipsis (...). Those three little dots are the key to varargs, and you'll be typing them quite often. Here's a version of the Guitar constructor that uses varargs to allow for an indeterminate number of String features:

```
public Guitar(String builder, String model, String... features);
```

All these constructors are shown, completed, in the source code for the com.oreilly.tiger.ch05.Guitar class.

The argument String... features indicates that any number of String arguments may be supplied. So all of the following invocations are legal:

```
Guitar guitar = new Guitar("Martin", "HD-28V",
                    "Hot-rodded by Dan Lashbrook", "Fossil Ivory Nut",
                    "Fossil Ivory Saddle", "Low-profile bridge pins");

Guitar guitar = new Guitar("Bourgeois", "OMC",
                    "Incredible flamed maple bindings on this one.");

Guitar guitar = new Guitar("Collings", "OM-42",
                    "Once owned by Steve Kaufman--one of a kind");
```

You could add the same variable-length argument to the other constructors:

```
public Guitar(String builder, String model,
            GuitarWood backSidesWood, GuitarWood topWood,
            float nutWidth, String... features)

public Guitar(String builder, String model,
            GuitarWood backSidesWood, GuitarWood topWood,
            float nutWidth,
            GuitarInlay fretboardInlay, GuitarInlay topInlay,
            String... features)
```

Example 5-1 shows a simple class that puts this all together, and even uses delegation to pass some varargs around.

Example 5-1. Using varargs in constructors

```
package com.oreilly.tiger.ch05;

public class Guitar {

  private String builder;
  private String model;
  private float nutWidth;
  private GuitarWood backSidesWood;
  private GuitarWood topWood;
  private GuitarInlay fretboardInlay;
  private GuitarInlay topInlay;

  private static final float DEFAULT_NUT_WIDTH = 1.6875f;

  public Guitar(String builder, String model, String... features) {
    this(builder, model, null, null, DEFAULT_NUT_WIDTH, null, null, features);
  }

  public Guitar(String builder, String model,
            GuitarWood backSidesWood, GuitarWood topWood,
            float nutWidth, String... features) {
    this(builder, model, backSidesWood, topWood, nutWidth, null, null, features);
```

Example 5-1. Using varargs in constructors (continued)

```
   }

   public Guitar(String builder, String model,
                 GuitarWood backSidesWood, GuitarWood topWood,
                 float nutWidth,
                 GuitarInlay fretboardInlay, GuitarInlay topInlay,
                 String... features) {

     this.builder = builder;
     this.model = model;
     this.backSidesWood = backSidesWood;
     this.topWood = topWood;
     this.nutWidth = nutWidth;
     this.fretboardInlay = fretboardInlay;
     this.topInlay = topInlay;
   }
}
```

What just happened?

When you specify a variable-length argument list, the Java compiler essentially reads that as "create an array of type *<argument type>*". You typed:

```
   public Guitar(String builder, String model, String... features)
```

However, the compiler interprets this as:

```
   public Guitar(String builder, String model, String[] features)
```

This means that iteration over the argument list is simple (as shown in "Iterating Over Variable-Length Argument Lists"), as is any other programming tasks you need to undertake. You can work with varargs just as you would with arrays.

You'll get a compiler error from this, and one that's not all that descriptive of the real problem.

However, there are some limitations. First, you can only use one ellipsis per method. Thus, the following is illegal:

```
   public Guitar(String builder, String model,
                 String... features, float... stringHeights)
```

Additionally, the ellipsis must appear as the *last* argument to a method.

What about...

...if you don't have any features to pass in? That's fine. Just call the constructor in the old way:

```
   Guitar guitar = new Guitar("Martin", "D-18");
```

Look closely, though—there is no constructor with the following signature:

```
public Guitar(String builder, String model)
```

So, what gives? Well, as an added bonus to varargs, *not* passing in an argument is a legitimate option. So when you see `String...` features, you should think "zero or more `String` arguments." That saves you from creating another constructor without the varargs parameter.

Iterating Over Variable-Length Argument Lists

All this varargs business is well and good, but unless you can actually use them in your methods, it's obviously just eye-candy and window dressing. However, you can work with vararg parameters just as you do an array, making usage a piece of cake.

How do I do that?

Make sure you read "Creating a Variable-Length Argument List," which lets you know the most important piece of information relating to vararg methods—variable-length arguments are treated just as arrays. So, continuing with the previous example, you could do something like this:

```
public Guitar(String builder, String model,
              GuitarWood backSidesWood, GuitarWood topWood,
              float nutWidth,
              GuitarInlay fretboardInlay, GuitarInlay topInlay,
              String... features) {

    this.builder = builder;
    this.model = model;
    this.backSidesWood = backSidesWood;
    this.topWood = topWood;
    this.nutWidth - nutWidth;
    this.fretboardInlay = fretboardInlay;
    this.topInlay = topInlay;

    for (String feature : features) {
      System.out.println(feature);
    }
  }
```

The for/in loop is covered in detail in Chapter 7.

This example is yanked straight out of Java in a Nutshell, Fifth Edition (O'Reilly).

This isn't particularly sexy, but it should get the point across. As another example, here's a simple method that calculates the maximum from a set of numbers:

```
      public static int max(int first, int... rest) {
        int max = first;
        for (int i : rest) {
          if (i > max)
            max = i;
        }
        return max;
      }
    }
```

Simple enough, right?

What about...

...storing variable-length arguments? Since the Java compiler treats these like arrays, an array is obviously a great choice for storage, as seen in Example 5-2, which is a modified version of Example 5-1.

Example 5-2. Storing variable-length arguments as member variables

```
package com.oreilly.tiger.ch05;

public class Guitar {

  private String builder;
  private String model;
  private float nutWidth;
  private GuitarWood backSidesWood;
  private GuitarWood topWood;
  private GuitarInlay fretboardInlay;
  private GuitarInlay topInlay;
  private String[] features;

  private static final float DEFAULT_NUT_WIDTH = 1.6875f;

  public Guitar(String builder, String model, String... features) {
    this(builder, model, null, null, DEFAULT_NUT_WIDTH, null, null, features);
  }

  public Guitar(String builder, String model,
               GuitarWood backSidesWood, GuitarWood topWood,
               float nutWidth, String... features) {
    this(builder, model, backSidesWood, topWood, nutWidth, null, null, features);
  }

  public Guitar(String builder, String model,
               GuitarWood backSidesWood, GuitarWood topWood,
               float nutWidth,
               GuitarInlay fretboardInlay, GuitarInlay topInlay,
               String... features) {
```

Example 5-2. Storing variable-length arguments as member variables (continued)

```
        this.builder = builder;
        this.model = model;
        this.backSidesWood = backSidesWood;
        this.topWood = topWood;
        this.nutWidth = nutWidth;
        this.fretboardInlay = fretboardInlay;
        this.topInlay = topInlay;
        this.features = features;
    }
}
```

You could also store these in Java collection classes easily:

```
// Variable declaration
private List features;

// Assignment in method or constructor body
this.features = java.util.Arrays.asList(features);
```

Allowing Zero-Length Argument Lists

One particularly nice feature about varargs is that a variable-length argument can take from *zero* to *n* arguments. This means that you can actually invoke one of these methods *without* any parameters, and things still behave. On the other hand, this means that, as a programmer, you better realize you must safeguard against this condition.

The java.util. Arrays class has several nice methods for working with arrays, all of which are of interest in varargs methods.

How do I do that?

Remember in "Iterating Over Variable-Length Argument Lists," you saw this simple method:

```
public static int max(int first, int... rest) {
    int max = first;
    for (int i : rest) {
        if (i > max)
            max = i;
    }
    return max;
}
```

You can call this method in several ways:

```
int max = MathUtils.max(1, 4);
int max = MathUtils.max(1, 2, 3, 4, 5, 6, 7, 8, 9, 10);
int max = MathUtils.max(18, 8, 4, 2, 1, 0);
```

What's not so nice is that there are many cases where you may already have the numbers to pass in stored as an array, or at least in some collected form:

```
// Get the numbers from some method
int[] numbers = getListOfNumbers();
```

It's impossible to just pass these numbers on to the max() method. You would need to check the list length, and strip off the first object (if it's available), then check the type to ensure it's an int. That would be passed in, along with the rest of the array (which can be iterated over, or converted manually to a suitable format). In general, this process is a real pain and is a lot of work for what should be trivial. To get around this, remember that this method is treated by the compiler as the following:

```
public static int max(int first, int[] rest)
```

So, by extension, you could convert max() to look like this:

```
public static int max(int... values) {
  int max = Integer.MIN_VALUE;
  for (int i : values) {
    if (i > max)
      max = i;
  }
  return max;
}
```

Autounboxing helps some, as "Integer" objects are freely converted to "int" primitives. Autounboxing is covered in Chapter 4.

You've now created a method that can easily be used with arrays:

```
// Get the numbers from some method
int[] numbers = getListOfNumbers();

int max = MathUtils.max(numbers);
```

While using a single variable-length argument made this task easier, it introduces problems if you pass in a zero-length array—in the best case, you're going to get unexpected results. To account for this, you now need a little error checking. Example 5-3 is a complete code listing for the MathUtils class, which at this point is more of a MathUtil class!

Example 5-3. Handling zero-argument methods

```
package com.oreilly.tiger.ch05;

public class MathUtils {

  public static int max(int... values) {
    if (values.length == 0) {
      throw new IllegalArgumentException("No values supplied.");
    }
```

Example 5-3. Handling zero-argument methods (continued)

```
    int max = Integer.MIN_VALUE;
    for (int i : values) {
      if (i > max)
        max = i;
    }
    return max;
  }
}
```

Anytime you have the possibility for a zero-length argument list, you need to perform this type of error checking. Generally, a nice informative IllegalArgumentException is a great solution.

Whatever you do, please don't throw a checked exception—you just add hassle for programmers using your code, and for what is a fringe case, rather than a normal problem.

What about...

...invoking this same method with normal non-array arguments? That's perfectly legal, of course. The following are all legitimate ways to invoke the max( ) method:

```
int max = MathUtils.max(myArray);
int max = MathUtils.max(new int[] { 2, 4, 6, 8 });
int max = MathUtils.max(2, 4, 6, 8);
int max = MathUtils.max(0);
int max = MathUtils.max( );
```

Specify Object Arguments Over Primitives

As discussed in Chapter 4, Tiger adds a variety of new features through *unboxing*. This allows you, in the case of varargs, to use object wrapper types in your method arguments.

How do I do that?

Remember that every class in Java ultimately is a descendant of java. lang.Object. This means that any object can be converted to an Object; further, because primitives like int and short are now automatically converted to their object wrapper types (Integer and Short in this case), *any* Java type can be converted to an Object.

Thus, if you want to accept the widest variety of argument types in your vararg methods, use an object type as the argument type. Better yet, go with Object for the absolute most in versatility. For example, take a method that did some printing:

```
private String print(Object... values) {
  StringBuilder sb = new StringBuilder();
  for (Object o : values) {
    sb.append(o)
      .append(" ");
  }
  return sb.toString();
}
```

The basic idea here is to print anything and everything. However, the more obvious way to declare this method is like this:

```
private String print(String... values) {
  StringBuilder sb = new StringBuilder();
  for (Object o : values) {
    sb.append(o)
      .append(" ");
  }
  return sb.toString();
}
```

The problem here is that now this method won't take Strings, ints, floats, arrays, and a variety of other types, all of which you might want to legitimately print.

By using a more general type, Object, you obtain the ability to print anything and everything.

Avoiding Automatic Array Conversion

Tiger adds all sorts of automatic conversions and conveniences, which is pretty cool...about 99% of the time. Unfortunately, there are times when all those helps turn into hindrances. The conversion of Object... to Object[] in a varargs method can be one of those cases, and you'll find that in rare cases, you need to work around Java.

How do I do that?

Before getting into the details of getting around this issue, be sure you understand the problem. Take Java's new printf() method, a real convenience:

```
System.out.printf("The balance of %s's account is $%(,6.2f\n",
             account.getOwner().getFullName(), account.getBalance());
```

printf( ), along
with the other
new Tiger format-
ting methods, are
detailed in
Chapter 9.

If you look at the Javadoc for `printf( )`, you'll see its a varargs method, with two parameters: a `String` for the formatting string, and then `Object...` for all the arguments passed in for use in that formatting string:

```
PrintStream printf(String format, Object... args)
```

By now, you can mentally convert this to the following:

```
PrintStream printf(String format, Object[] args)
```

All good, right? Well, most of the time. Consider the following code:

```
Object[] objectArray = getObjectArrayFromSomewhereElse( );
out.printf("Description of object array: %s\n", obj);
```

I realize this isn't
the most common
scenario. Then
again, if all I
covered were
common scenar-
ios, we'd all be
debugging right
now, wouldn't we?

This might seem a bit far-fetched—however, consider this as normal fare for *introspective code*. That's a ten-cent word for code that investigates other code. If you are writing a code analysis tool, or an IDE, or anything else that might use reflection or a similar API to figure out what objects an application uses, this suddenly becomes a normal usecase. Here, you're not really interested in the contents of the object array as much as you are with the array itself. What type is it? What's its memory address? What is its `String` representation? Keep in mind that all these questions apply to the array itself, and *not* to the contents of the array. For example, let's say the array is something like this:

```
public Object[] getObjectArrayFromSomewhereElse( ) {
  return new String[] {"Hello", "to", "all", "of", "you"};
}
```

In that case, you might write some code like this to begin to answer some questions about this array:

```
out.printf("Description of object array: %s\n", obj);
```

However, the output isn't what you expect:

```
run-ch05:
    [echo] Running Chapter 5 examples from Java Tiger: A Developer's
Notebook

    [echo] Running VarargsTester...
    [java] Hello
```

What in the world? This is hardly what you'd expect to see—however, the compiler did just what it always did—it converted `Object...` in the `printf( )` method to `Object[]`. When it read your method invocation, it saw an argument that was, in fact, `Object[]`! So instead of treating the array as an object itself, it broke it up into its various parts. The first argument became the `String` "Hello", which was passed to the format string (%s), and the result was "Hello" being printed out.

To get around this, you need to tell the compiler that you want the entire object array, obj, treated as a *single* object, and not as a grouping of arguments. Here's the magic bullet:

```
out.printf("Description of object array: %s\n", new Object[] { obj });
```

Alternatively, here's an even shorter approach:

```
out.printf("Description of object array: %s\n", (Object)obj);
```

In both cases, the compiler no longer sees an array of objects, it simply sees a single Object (which just happens to be an array of objects). The result is what you should want (at least in this rather odd scenario):

```
run-ch05:
     [echo] Running Chapter 5 examples from Java Tiger: A Developer's
Notebook

     [echo] Running VarargsTester...
     [java] [Ljava.lang.String;@c44b88
```

While this may look like gibberish to you, it's probably what reflection-based or other introspective code wants to take a look at.

CHAPTER 6

Annotations

One of the more popular terms being tossed around in programming these days is *metadata*. Metadata is simply information about information. It resides somewhere in the spectrum between Java source code, which is raw information for a compiler, and JavadocJavadoc, which is pure documentation. Metadata typically makes statements about source code that is interpreted at some point, usually by a code or data analysis tool.

Your first thought might be, "Well, Javadoc takes care of that, right?" Consider this—how many ways are there to say, "This variable should not be null." In Javadoc, you might say "non-null," you might say "This variable shouldn't be null," you might say "Don't assign null to this." All are valid in terms of documentation, but there is no consistency among them. There isn't any tool that could analyze and account for all the variances in how you might state this simple condition. Annotations, new to Tiger, seek to solve that problem by providing a well-defined metadata mechanism.

In a nutshell, annotations are modifiers that can be applied to package and type declarations, constructors, methods, fields, parameters, and even variables. They take the form of *name=value* pairs, and you can use Java's built-in types, as well as define custom annotation types of your own.

Using Standard Annotation Types

Standard annotation types are those that are provided "out of the box" in Tiger. There are three of these, and all three are defined in the java.lang package. These annotation types can be used without any extra work on your part in your own programs.

How do I do that?

The three standard annotation types that are pre-defined in Tiger are listed here, detailed briefly, and then covered more fully in the following labs:

Override

    java.lang.Override is used to indicate that a method overrides a method in its superclass.

Deprecated

    java.lang.Deprecated indicates that use of a method or element type is discouraged.

SuppressWarnings

    java.lang.SuppressWarnings turns off compiler warnings for classes, methods, or field and variable initializers..

None of these have to be imported, as they are all in the "java.lang" package, and are automatically available.

Here's an example of using the Override annotation type:

```
@Override
public String toString() {
  return super.toString() + " [modified by subclass]";
}
```

Here's a sample of using Deprecated:

```
@Deprecated public class Betamax { ... }
```

And finally, here's SuppressWarnings in action:

```
@SuppressWarnings("unchecked")
public void nastyMethod() {
  // body omitted
}
```

I realize that I really haven't told you how these work—that's intentional. Now that you've seen each annotation in use, you should realize that each has an entirely different syntax. To get a handle on annotations, we'll have to delve into just a bit of theory, and then there are labs going into each of the standard annotations in detail. Buckle up for a moment, let's deal with some technical details, and then you'll be ready for some more practical instruction.

What just happened?

First, you need to understand the difference between an *annotation* and an *annotation type*. Taking the last part first, an annotation type is a specific name of an annotation, along with any default values and related information. You just saw three annotation types: Override, Deprecated, and SuppressWarnings. An annotation, then, uses an annotation type to associate some piece of information with a Java program element (methods, classes, variables, etc.). So your code might only use one annotation type, like Override, and yet have ten or fifteen annotations (if it used Override ten or fifteen times).

Annotation types can have values as well—note that SuppressWarnings passed in the valued "unchecked", which would be used by the annotation type to process or store information. This passed-in value, along with any default values, all make up the annotation's *members*. This is where the *name=value* syntax comes in that I mentioned in the early part of this lab—it allows for an annotation's members to be set.

In addition to the three standard annotation types, there are three categories of annotations:

Marker annotations

Marker annotations are used with annotation types that define no members. They simply provide information contained within the name of the annotation itself. An annotation whose members all have default values can also be used as a marker, since no information must be passed in. The syntax of a marker is simply:

```
@MarkerAnnotation
```

Single-value annotations

Single-value annotations have just a single member, named value. The format of a single-value annotation is:

```
@SingleValueAnnotation("some value")
```

There are no semicolons at the end of annotation lines.

Full annotations

A full annotation really isn't a category, as much as it is an annotation type that uses the full range of annotation syntax. Here parentheses follow the annotation name, and all members are assigned values:

```
@Reviews({  // Curly braces indicate an array of values
   @Review(grade=Review.Grade.EXCELLENT, reviewer="df"),
   @Review(grade=Review.Grade.UNSATISFACTORY, reviewer="eg",
        comment="This method needs an @Override annotation")
})
```

With each category, there is a slightly different syntax—which is why each standard annotation type is used a little differently. Each of the following three labs will detail one of the standard annotation types, indicate the category it falls into, and give you further details about using that annotation type.

What about...

...tools like XDoclet (*http://xdoclet.sourceforge.net*) that already handle this sort of analysis, especially in enterprise programming. XDoclet already provides for much of the same information, reading metadata in source code and managing dependences (especially between the numerous source file listings required for EJBs), all through Javadoc parsing and some nifty class generation tools.

These tools are actually great examples of why annotations are needed. While XDoclet parses Javadoc, it can't figure out if the Javadoc syntax is correct or not—if it finds matching tags, it uses them, and a misspelling is ignored without a peep. However, annotations are checked by the Java compiler—meaning you can't have something like this in your code:

```
@Overridde  // Note the misspelling
```

The compiler will complain about this misspelling, meaning you're protected not only at the code level, but at the annotation level as well. Now, take this extra checking, and pair it with the associations, analysis, and code generation that XDoclet does. Suddenly, a great tool becomes even better, even more user-friendly, even more a part of the standard suite of Java tools. In short, annotations could be the real breakthrough in making tools such as XDoclet a part of every programmer's toolkit.

Annotating an Overriding Method

The Override annotation type is a marker interface, and has no members to initialize. It is used to indicate that a method is overriding a method from its superclass. In particular, it's supposed to help ensure you actually *do* override a method—by avoiding misspellings or confusion over the correct name and parameter list of the method you're trying to override. In these cases of error, a compiler can catch the problem and report it.

How do I do that?

Because Override is a marker interface, there are no values that you need to supply it. Just preface it with the annotation syntax marker, the at sign (@), and type "Override". This should be on a line by itself, just before the method declaration you want to indicate as an overriding method, as seen in Example 6-1.

Largely by coincidence, the @ sign, pronounced "at", is a mnemonic for Annotation Type.

Example 6-1. Using the Override annotation type

```
package com.oreilly.tiger.ch06;

public class OverrideTester {

  public OverrideTester() { }

  @Override
  public String toString() {
    return super.toString() + " [OverrideTester Implementation]";
  }

  @Override
  public int hashCode() {
    return toString().hashCode();
  }
}
```

This isn't very sexy or glamorous, but it compiles without any problem. Where things start to become useful is when you *don't* do what you intended do. Change the hashCode() method to look like this:

This method exists, but is commented out of, the Override-Tester's source listing in the book's sample code.

```
@Override
public int hasCode() {
  return toString().hashCode();
}
```

Here, hashCode() is misspelled, and the method is no longer overriding anything, making the annotation speak up. Compile this class, and you'll get the following error:

```
[javac] src\ch06\OverrideTester.java:1:
            method does not override a method from its superclass
[javac]   @Override
[javac]    ^
[javac] 1 error
```

Suddenly, that little annotation becomes quite a boon, catching mistakes at compile time. It's also such an easy thing to integrate into your programming practices that I'd recommend you use it often.

What about...

...the methods that *should be* overridden? Override marks the *overriding* method, not the *overridden* method—this is an important distinction, and you should learn it well. Java has ways to indicate that a method should be overridden already—namely, by declaring that method as abstract.

Annotating a Deprecated Method

Like Override, java.lang.Deprecated is a marker annotation type. It also has an analog in the Javadoc world, the @deprecated tag. Both indicate the same thing, although to different tools (see the "What about..." section). Use Deprecated anytime you want to ensure that classes are warned about overriding a particular method.

How do I do that?

Deprecated is a marker interface, and is used without parentheses or member values, just as Override is. However, it is intended to be placed on the same line as the declaration that is deprecated, where the Override annotation was placed on the prior line. Example 6-2 is a simple example of using Deprecated.

Example 6-2. Using the Deprecated annotation type

```
package com.oreilly.tiger.ch06;

public class DeprecatedClass {

  /**
   * This method has now been deprecated in favor of doSomethingElse()
   * @deprecated Use doSomethingElse() instead
   */
  @Deprecated public void doSomething() {
    // Really... do something...
  }

  public void doSomethingElse() {
    // Do something else (and presumably better)
  }
}
```

On its own, this annotation doesn't do anything. However, it comes into play when other classes override deprecated methods, as the class in Example 6-3 does.

Example 6-3. Overriding a method marked as deprecated

```
package com.oreilly.tiger.ch06;

public class DeprecatedTester extends DeprecatedClass {

  public void doSomething() {
```

Example 6-3. Overriding a method marked as deprecated (continued)

```
    // Overrides a deprecated method
  }
}
```

If you compile these classes, and turn on deprecation checking in your compiler, you'll get a warning:

```
[javac] src\ch06\DeprecatedTester.java:5: warning:
        [deprecation] doSomething() in
          com.oreilly.tiger.ch06.DeprecatedClass has been deprecated
[javac]   public void doSomething() {
[javac]               ^
```

Again, this isn't a revolutionary new feature, but it still adds some help for introspection tools such as XDoclet.

What about...

...the @deprecated Javadoc tag? First, realize that it's not at all made obsolete by the Deprecated annotation type. Javadoc comments are consumed by the Javadoc tool, and are a vital part of any class's documentation. The Deprecated annotation type is then used by the compiler to ensure that your code matches what the documentation indicates—that a method or class is indeed deprecated. It's an important distinction, and well worth remembering. In fact, you should *always* use the two in tandem, one for documentation and one for compilation. Additionally, the compiler will still read and process the @deprecated tag for backwards compatibility.

In addition, you might wonder about the -deprecation flag, also available to be passed to javac. If you compile with the -deprecation flag, but without -Xlint:deprecation, you get the exact same result as using -Xlint:deprecation. In fact, from what I can tell from testing the JDK, these two flags function identically in Tiger.

Suppressing Warnings

With the advent of Tiger, there are times when pre-Tiger code works exactly as it should, but generates warnings. This is most often the case in collections, as Tiger allows much stronger typing, and in fact pushes you to code that way. However, thoroughly tested code should never issue or generate warnings, creating a bit of a catch 22. Your code works great, but causes warnings in Tiger—on the other hand, ignoring *all* warnings in a program isn't a good idea, either. How do you deal with this situation?

Turn on deprecation checking with the "-Xlint: deprecation" flag.

The Javadoc tag is lower-case, the annotation type is uppercase.

You can view warnings from the Java compiler with the "-Xlint" switch.

The answer is to use another standard annotation type, SuppressWarnings, which lets you turn off warnings for a particular class, method, or field/variable initializer. At the same time, warnings for other pieces of code are left intact, as they should be.

How do I do that?

SuppressWarnings is not a marker interface, as Deprecated and Override are, but instead has a single member named value. value is a String array (String[]), and the value of this member is an array of the types of warnings to be suppressed. So, you could suppress unchecked warnings with the following annotation:

```
/**
 * Normal pre-Tiger method body
 */
@SuppressWarnings(value={"unchecked"})
public void nonGenericsMethod( ) {
  List wordList = new ArrayList( );

  wordList.add("foo");
}
```

If you're used to looking at Tiger code, you may see something wrong here—because generics aren't used, this generates an unchecked warning (at least, without the SuppressWarnings annotation) because wordList is untyped. However, this warning disappears with the annotation—particularly useful if you're compiling under Tiger, but targeting a pre-Tiger platform.

If you remove the annotation, you can see the warning that this code generates:

```
[javac] src\ch06\SuppressWarningsTester.java:15:
   warning: [unchecked] unchecked call to add(E) as a member of the
            raw type java.util.List
[javac]     wordList.add("foo");
[javac]            ^
```

Of course, this has no business showing up if you truly are merely trying to target a pre-Tiger platform, and it's here that SuppressWarnings really comes into play. You can also specify multiple warnings to ignore:

```
/**
 * Normal pre-Tiger method body
 */
@Suppres                          "  lthrough"})
public
  List

  wordL
}
```

An example of a warning that should be fixed is not handling all enumerated type values in a "switch" statement.

This code is in com.oreilly.tiger.ch06.SuppressWarnings Tester.

In fact, there's one more notation step you can take—annotation types that only have one member will automatically pass all values through to that member, as long as that member is named value. As a result, you can omit the value= portion of the declaration:

<aside>Curly braces are used anytime a member takes an array of values.</aside>

```
/**
 * Normal pre-Tiger method body
 */
@SuppressWarnings({"unchecked", "fallthrough"})
public void nonGenericsMethod() {
  List wordList = new ArrayList();

  wordList.add("foo");
}
```

This is a nice keystroke saver, at least in my book. The compiler is smart enough to route these values to the annotation type's single member, value.

Creating Custom Annotation Types

While the three annotation types you've seen are useful, they hardly cover all the types of annotations you may want to make on your source code. In fact, you may get so into annotations that you want to define some of your own. Fortunately, Tiger lets you do this with the @interface keyword, along with a few other oddball syntactical constructs new to the language.

How do I do that?

Annotation types are, at their most basic level, Java interfaces. As such, they look similar to a normal Java interface definition, but you use the @interface keyword instead of interface, which tells the compiler that you're writing an annotation type instead of a normal interface. Example 6-4 is a very simple marker interface.

Example 6-4. Simple marker annotation type

```
package com.oreilly.tiger.ch06;

/**
 * Marker annotation to indicate that a method or class
 *   is still in progress.
 */
public @interface InProgress { }
```

You can use this on any method or class you like:

```
@com.oreilly.tiger.ch06.InProgress
public void calculateInterest(float amount, float rate) {
    // Need to finish this method later
}
```

You can define an annotation type with a member nearly as easily, as Example 6-5 illustrates.

Example 6-5. An annotation with a member

```
package com.oreilly.tiger.ch06;

/**
 * Annotation type to indicate a task still needs to
 *    be completed.
 */
public @interface TODO {
  String value();
}
```

In this example, you don't need to prefix "InProgress" with its package, but it illustrates that these are used just like other Java classes.

The declaration of the member is simple enough, but the parenthesis at the end probably looks a little odd—that's because it's not just a member declaration, but also a *method* declaration. You're actually defining a method called value( ), and the compiler then automatically creates a member variable with the same name. Along the same lines, since annotation types function like interfaces, the methods are all implicitly abstract, and have no bodies.

The variable name value is used, which lets source code that references this type use the shorthand notation @TODO(*stringValue*). This is a nice feature, and one you should strive to allow for. You see all of this in play in the following:

```
@com.oreilly.tiger.ch06.InProgress
@TODO("Figure out the amount of interest per month")
public void calculateInterest(float amount, float rate) {
    // Need to finish this method later
}
```

Oddly enough, the Java folks didn't go with the tried-and-true JavaBeans conventions, with methods like setXXX( ) and getXXX( ).

Adding an extra member (or two) is equally simple, as Example 6-6 demonstrates.

Example 6-6. Multiple members in an annotation type

```
package com.oreilly.tiger.ch06;

public @interface GroupTODO {
```

This is really an amped-up version of "TODO", shown in Example 6-5.

Example 6-6. *Multiple members in an annotation type (continued)*

```
public enum Severity { CRITICAL, IMPORTANT, TRIVIAL, DOCUMENTATION };

Severity severity( ) default Severity.IMPORTANT;
String item( );
String assignedTo( );
}
```

Here, an enumerated type is added to spice up the mix, and then used by the `severity` member. `item` still holds the item that needs to be handled, and `assignedTo` provides the person the TODO item is assigned to:

Chapter 3 covers enumerated types.

```
@com.oreilly.tiger.ch06.InProgress
@GroupTODO(
    severity=GroupTODO.Severity.CRITICAL,
    item="Figure out the amount of interest per month",
    assignedTo="Brett McLaughlin"
)
public void calculateInterest(float amount, float rate) {
    // Need to finish this method later
}
```

As a final note, you can set member values to defaults, although the syntax looks more than a little odd; Example 6-7 is an updated version of Example 6-6.

Example 6-7. *Default values in an annotation type*

```
package com.oreilly.tiger.ch06;

import java.util.Date;

public @interface GroupTODO {

  public enum Severity { CRITICAL, IMPORTANT, TRIVIAL, DOCUMENTATION };

  Severity severity( ) default Severity.IMPORTANT;
  String item( );
  String assignedTo( );
  String dateAssigned( );
}
```

This is probably even stranger for me to type than the new generics syntax, so it may take some time to get used to. Still, it's nice to be able to set these defaults, even if it is a little syntactically strange.

What about...

...extending other interfaces, or even annotation types? You can't. The `@interface` keyword implicitly indicates an extension of `java.lang.`

annotation.Annotation—and you can't compile an annotation type that explicitly tries to extend anything else. However, you can extend and implement annotation types, although these extensions and implementations are *not* treated as annotation types.

Annotating Annotations

Just as you can annotate classes, you can also annotate your own custom annotations. This may seem a little silly at first blush, but if you begin to build up a large repository of customized notations, this becomes quite important. Just as Javadoc and comments are incredibly useful for a programmer studying a previously written class, *meta-annotations*, or annotations on annotations, are indispensable for figuring out someone else's intent for a customized annotation.

How do I do that?

There are four standard meta-annotations, all defined in the java.lang. annotation package:

Target
> This meta-annotation specifies which program elements can have annotations of the defined type.

Retention
> This meta-annotation indicates whether an annotation is tossed out by the compiler, or retained in the compiled class file. In cases where the annotation is retained, it also specifies whether it is read by the Java virtual machine at class load.

Documented
> This meta-annotation indicates that the defined annotation should be considered as part of the public API of the annotated program element.

Inherited
> This meta-annotation is intended for use on annotation types that are targeted at classes, indicating that the annotated type is an inherited one.

These are all somewhat self-explanatory, so with a few examples, these meta-annotations should be easy to put into use. Each is covered in detail in the next several labs.

Defining an Annotation Type's Target

The first meta-annotation, Target, is used to specify which program elements are allowed as targets for the defined annotation. This prevents misuse of an annotation, and is strongly recommended as a sanity check for all your custom annotations.

How do I do that?

Target should be used in the lines directly preceding the annotation definition:

```
@Target({ElementType.TYPE,
         ElementType.METHOD,
         ElementType.CONSTRUCTOR,
         ElementType.ANNOTATION_TYPE})
public @interface TODO {
```

The actual parameter type in Target is ElementType[].

Target takes a single member whose type is an array of values, each of which should be an enumerated value from the java.lang.annotation. ElementType enum.

This enum defines the various program elements allowed as targets of an annotation type, and is shown in Example 6-8.

Example 6-8. The ElementType enum

```
package java.lang.annotation;

public enum ElementType {
  TYPE,              // Class, interface, or enum (but not annotation)
  FIELD,             // Field (including enumerated values)
  METHOD,            // Method (does not include constructors)
  PARAMETER,         // Method parameter
  CONSTRUCTOR,       // Constructor
  LOCAL_VARIABLE,    // Local variable or catch clause
  ANNOTATION_TYPE,   // Annotation Types (meta-annotations)
  PACKAGE            // Java Package
}
```

You'll need to remember to import both Target and ElementType in your code. Example 6-9 shows an updated version of the TODO annotation type, first defined back in Example 6-5.

Example 6-9. Annotating an annotation

```
package com.oreilly.tiger.ch06;

import java.lang.annotation.ElementType;
```

Example 6-9. Annotating an annotation (continued)

```
import java.lang.annotation.Target;

/**
 * Annotation type to indicate a task still needs to
 *    be completed.
 */
@Target({ElementType.TYPE,
         ElementType.METHOD,
         ElementType.CONSTRUCTOR,
         ElementType.ANNOTATION_TYPE})
public @interface TODO {
  String value();
}
```

It's interesting to note the Target meta-annotation is used on itself (shown in Example 6-10), indicating that it can only be used as a meta-annotation.

Example 6-10. Source code for Target annotation type

```
package java.lang.annotation;

@Documented
@Retention(RetentionPolicy.RUNTIME);
@Target(ElementType.ANNOTATION_TYPE)
public @interface Target {
  ElementType[] value();
}
```

What about...

...annotation types that work for all program elements? In these cases, you don't need to use Target at all.

Setting the Retention of an Annotation Type

The Retention meta-annotation annotation defines how the Java compiler treats annotations. Annotations can be tossed out of a compiled class file by the compiler, or kept in the class file. Additionally, the Java virtual machine can ignore annotations (when they are retained in the class file), or read those annotations at the time a class is first loaded. All of these options are specified by Retention.

A few folks recommend using Target and indicating all valid ElementTypes for documentation purposes. I think this is pretty silly, to be honest.

How do I do that?

Like Target, you specify the retention of an annotation type just before the annotation definition (the public @interface line). Also, like Target, the argument to Retention must be a value from an enum support class—in this case, java.lang.annotation.RetentionPolicy. This enum is shown in Example 6-11.

Example 6-11. The RetentionPolicy enum

```
package java.lang.annotation;

public enum RetentionPolicy {
   SOURCE,        // Annotation is discarded by the compiler
   CLASS,         // Annotation is stored in the class file, but ignored by the VM
   RUNTIME        // Annotation is stored in the class file and read by the VM
}
```

The default retention policy, for all annotations, is RetentionPolicy. CLASS. This retains annotations, but doesn't require the VM to read them when classes are loaded.

Don't forget to import java.lang. annotation. Retention and java.lang.annotation.Retention Policy.

A good example of using Retention occurs in the SuppressWarnings annotation. As that annotation type is purely used for compilation (ensuring warnings of the specified type are suppressed), it does not need to be retained in a class's bytecode:

```
@Retention(RetentionPolicy.SOURCE)
public @interface SuppressWarnings {
```

Documenting Annotation Types

Annotations are a nice addition, and are a particularly cool feature if you need to troubleshoot, update, or maintain code that was written by someone else. It also makes for a killer code-level management system on open source projects. In "Creating Custom Annotation Types," I developed very simple annotation types—InProgress, TODO, and GroupTODO—that would all function in that sort of environment. While these are great if you're actually scanning source code, they aren't visible in the code's Javadoc. This is where the Documented meta-annotation comes into play. You can use it to ensure your annotations show up in generated Javadoc.

If you're using the supplied Ant buildfile, use "ant Javadoc" to generate Javadoc.

How do I do that?

First, to understand what detail you are missing *without* using Documented, generate Javadoc for the source code of this book. Pull up those API docs, and navigate to the `com.oreilly.tiger.ch06` package, and then the `AnnotationTester` class. Scroll down, if needed, to the `calculateInterest()` method—you should see something similar to Figure 6-1.

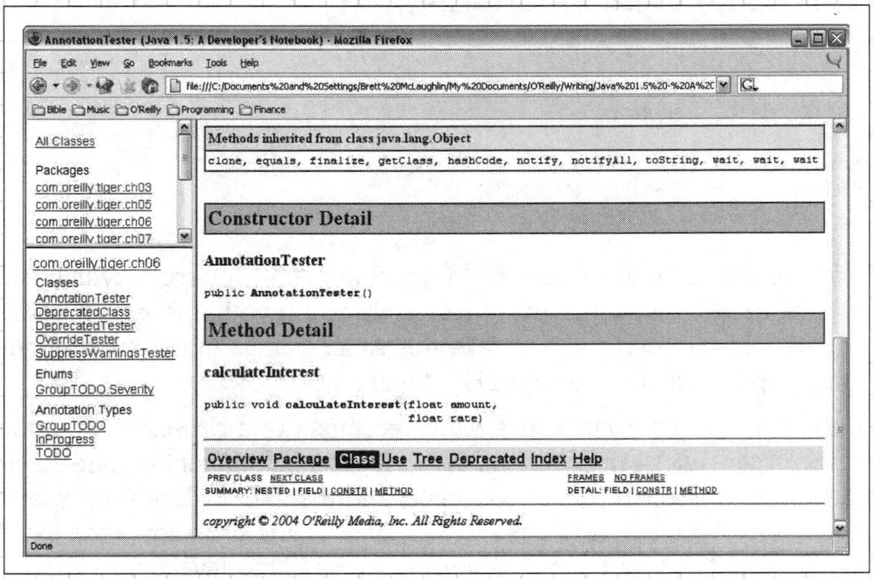

Figure 6-1. calculateInterest( ) without documentation of annotations

Nothing special, right? Right—but there's something missing. Remember the code for this method:

```
@com.oreilly.tiger.ch06.InProgress
@GroupTODO(
    severity=GroupTODO.Severity.CRITICAL,
    item="Figure out the amount of interest per month",
    assignedTo="Brett McLaughlin",
    dateAssigned="04-26-2004"
)
public void calculateInterest(float amount, float rate) {
    // Need to finish this method later
}
```

While the source code contains some pretty important information, in the form of the `InProgress` and `GroupTODO` annotations, this information is missing from the Javadoc.

To fix this, you need to add a `@Documented` meta-annotation to any annotation type that you want to appear in Javadoc. In this case, both `InProgress` and `GroupTODO`, as well as `TODO`, could use this addition. Example 6-12 shows an updated `InProgress`; you can add the same lines to the other annotation types.

Example 6-12. Adding documentation to InProgress

```
package com.oreilly.tiger.ch06;

import java.lang.annotation.Documented;
import java.lang.annotation.Retention;
import java.lang.annotation.RetentionPolicy;

/**
 * Marker annotation to indicate that a method or class
 *   is still in progress.
 */
@Documented
@Retention(RetentionPolicy.RUNTIME)
public @interface InProgress { }
```

I've also added the Retention meta-annotation to this class; anytime you use the Documented annotation, you should pair it with a retention policy of RetentionPolicy.RUNTIME. Make this same change to the other annotation types defined in com.oreilly.tiger.ch03.

"ant clean" will remove all compiled class files, and Javadoc files, allowing a clean generation of Javadoc.

Clean out your old Javadoc files. Now, recompile your classes and run the Javadoc generator again. This time, you'll get a bit different output—navigate again to com.oreilly.tiger.ch06, and then AnnotationTester, and finally to the calculateInterest( ) method. Figure 6-2 shows the same method, but this time the annotations show up in the Javadoc.

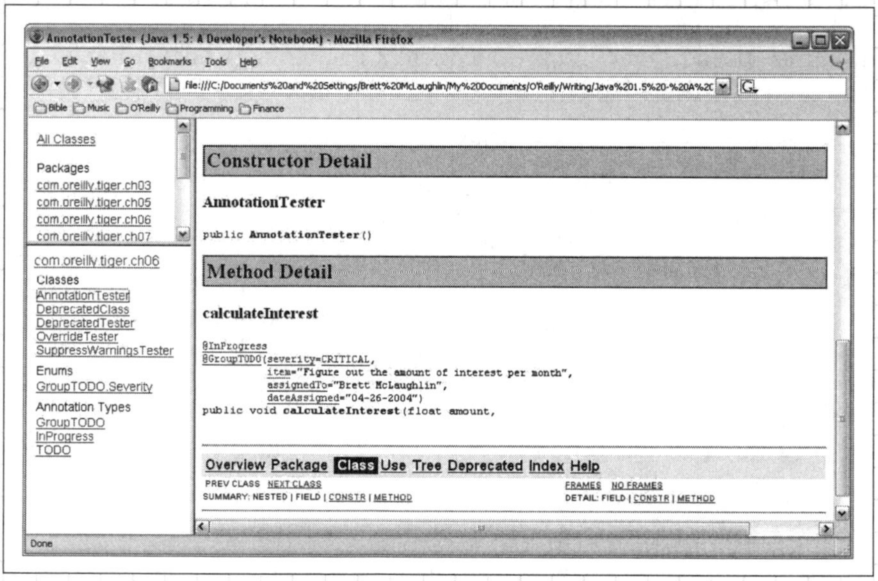

Figure 6-2. Javadoc with annotations showing up

Setting Up Inheritance in Annotations

A classic case of creating a problematic situation comes up with inheritance. Consider a class that has been deprecated, and set to be phased out of use. It's possible (and quite easy) for a programmer who isn't paying attention to extend that class, use it all over the place, and avoid the deprecated warnings that would have shown up if the superclass, which *is* deprecated, was used. The problem is that a class that is deprecated doesn't pass on this deprecation status to its subclasses—creating a potential for real problems in your code. Suddenly you have thousands of references to a non-deprecated class, but you can't remove the deprecated class because it's the superclass of all the referenced objects! Using the Inherited meta-annotation can help out here.

How do I do that?

Let's take another example of a status, represented by an annotation, which should be inherited: the InProgress indicator. Example 6-13 shows a simple class that uses this annotation.

Example 6-13. Using the InProgress annotation

```
package com.oreilly.tiger.ch06;

import java.io.IOException;
import java.io.PrintStream;

@InProgress
public class Super {

  public void print(PrintStream out) throws IOException {
    out.println("Super printing...");
  }
}
```

Example 6-14 is another simple class, which extends Super.

Example 6-14. Extending the Super class

```
package com.oreilly.tiger.ch06;

import java.io.IOException;
import java.io.PrintStream;

public class Sub extends Super {
```

Example 6-14. Extending the Super class (continued)

```
  public void print(PrintStream out) throws IOException {
    out.println("Sub printing...");
  }
}
```

If you generate the Javadoc for these classes, you'll see, as shown in Figure 6-3, that Super is correctly noted as being in progress.

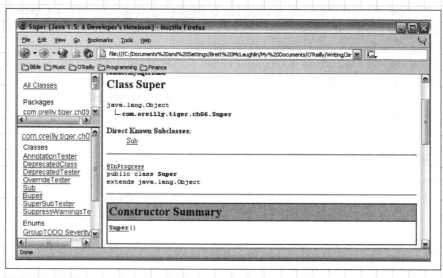

Figure 6-3. Super, with an InProgress annotation

The problem is that Sub, which is based on an in-progress class, does *not* have this indicator (see Figure 6-4).

The problem is that the InProgress annotation type isn't inherited; this use-case shows that's probably a mistake. To correct it, make the following change to InProgress:

```
  @Documented
  @Inherited
  @Retention(RetentionPolicy.RUNTIME)
  public @interface InProgress { }
```

Recompile your classes, and re-generate your Javadoc. I'll bet you're expecting to see another figure, with the Sub class pulled up, flagged as being in progress. Well, that's what I was expecting too—but it doesn't work yet. Presumably this will be fixed before things go final, but hopefully you've at least gotten the idea about what *should* happen.

It's also worth noting that while the documentation feature isn't working correctly, reflection is. You can indeed determine that Sub is in progress

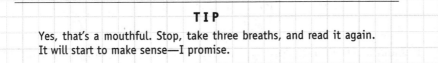

Figure 6-4. Sub, without an annotation

through reflection—it just doesn't show up in the Javadoc. To see how reflection works with annotations, see "Reflecting on Annotations".

What about...

...interfaces? Annotations marked as Inherited only apply to subclasses, so implementing a method with annotations will *not* result in the annotations being inherited.

Additionally, if you override a method from a superclass, you don't inherit that specific method's annotations. Only the annotations on the superclass itself are inherited, and those by the subclass as a whole.

TIP

Yes, that's a mouthful. Stop, take three breaths, and read it again. It will start to make sense—I promise.

Reflecting on Annotations

So far, all the discussions on annotations have been around looking at them visually—either in source code or in Javadoc. However, there are enough code introspection tools these days that it's worth talking about using reflection to determine what annotations a class (or field, or method) has. The java.lang.reflect package has several additions that make this a piece of cake.

How do I do that?

The easiest way to check for an annotation is by using the isAnnotationPresent() method. This lets you specify the annotation to check for, and get a true/false result:

This code is in the ReflectionTester class.

```java
public void testAnnotationPresent(PrintStream out) throws IOException {
    Class c = Super.class;
    boolean inProgress = c.isAnnotationPresent(InProgress.class);
    if (inProgress) {
        out.println("Super is In Progress");
    } else {
        out.println("Super is not In Progress");
    }
}
```

Running this code gives you the following output:

```
run-ch06:
    [echo] Running Chapter 6 examples from Java Tiger: A Developer's
Notebook
    [echo] Running ReflectionTester...
    [java] Super is In Progress
```

Additionally, this approach lets you take advantage of the Inherited annotation, described in "Setting Up Inheritance in Annotations":

This assumes you follow the steps in "Setting Up Inheritance in Annotations" and mark "Super" as being in progress.

```java
public void testInheritedAnnotation(PrintStream out) throws IOException {
    Class c = Sub.class;
    boolean inProgress = c.isAnnotationPresent(InProgress.class);
    if (inProgress) {
        out.println("Sub is In Progress");
    } else {
        out.println("Sub is not In Progress");
    }
}
```

Remember that although Sub is not marked as in progress, it inherits from Super, which is in progress. Additionally, the InProgress annotation was marked as Inherited, so the in-progress indicator should be passed on to subclasses. Running this new method shows that this, indeed, works:

```
run-ch06:
    [echo] Running Chapter 6 examples from Java Tiger: A Developer's
Notebook
    [echo] Running VarargsTester...
    [java] Super is In Progress
    [java] Sub is In Progress
```

Although this is not picked up in the Javadoc, it certainly appears in your reflection-based code.

If you're not checking for a marker interface, though, you may have to go beyond isAnnotationPresent( )—especially if you need to get values from the annotation. Here's a simple example:

```
public void testGetAnnotation(PrintStream out)
  throws IOException, NoSuchMethodException {

  Class c = AnnotationTester.class;
  MethodElement element = c.getMethod("calculateInterest",
                            float.class, float.class);

  GroupTODO groupTodo = element.getAnnotation(GroupTODO.class);
  String assignedTo = groupTodo.assignedTo( );

  out.println("TODO Item on Annotation Tester is assigned to: '" +
    assignedTo + "'");
}
```

Reflection on annotations only works for annotation types that have Runtime retention.

Once the method in question is located (in this case, calculateInterest( ) on the AnnotationTester class), that method can be queried for a specific annotation. In this case, the code locates the GroupTODO annotation, and grabs the value of assignedTo. The output of this method is shown here:

```
run-ch06:
     [echo] Running Chapter 6 examples from Java Tiger: A Developer's
Notebook

     [echo] Running ReflectionTester...
     [java] Super is In Progress
     [java] Sub is In Progress
     [java] TODO Item on Annotation Tester is assigned to: 'Brett
McLaughlin'
```

To use this code, you obviously have to know exactly what you're looking for—and that's one of the few drawbacks of getAnnotation( ).

Finally, you can use getAnnotations( ) if you're trying to locate *all* annotations for a program element, or if you need to iterate through all annotations looking for a specific one. For example, here's a simple utility method that prints out all annotations for a supplied element:

```
public void printAnnotations(AnnotatedElement e, PrintStream out)
  throws IOException {

  out.printf("Printing annotations for '%s'%n%n", e.toString( ));

  Annotation[] annotations = e.getAnnotations( );
  for (Annotation a : annotations) {
```

The for/in loop is detailed in Chapter 7, and printf( ) and other new formatting methods are covered in Chapter 9.

```
                    out.printf("    * Annotation '%s' found%n",
                        a.annotationType().getName());
            }
        }
```

If you supplied this method the calculateInterest() method from
AnnotationTester, you'd get the following output:

```
run-ch06:
    [echo] Running Chapter 6 examples from Java Tiger: A Developer's
Notebook
    [echo] Running ReflectionTester...
    [java] Super is In Progress
    [java] Sub is In Progress
    [java] TODO Item on Annotation Tester is assigned to: 'Brett
McLaughlin'
    [java] Printing annotations for 'public void com.oreilly.tiger.ch06.
Annotat
ionTester.calculateInterest(float,float)'

    [java]      * Annotation 'com.oreilly.tiger.ch06.InProgress' found
    [java]      * Annotation 'com.oreilly.tiger.ch06.GroupTODO' found
```

This code is really pretty straightforward, so I'll leave it to you to work
through the details. Example 6-15 is the complete code listing for
ReflectionTester, which has all these reflection-based annotation
methods within it.

*If you don't want to pick up inherited annotations, you can use get
DeclaredAnnotations() instead of getAnnotations().*

Example 6-15. Testing reflection-based annotation methods

```java
package com.oreilly.tiger.ch06;

import java.io.IOException;
import java.io.PrintStream;
import java.lang.reflect.AnnotatedElement;
import java.lang.annotation.Annotation;

public class ReflectionTester {

  public ReflectionTester() {
  }

  public void testAnnotationPresent(PrintStream out) throws IOException {
    Class c = Super.class;
    boolean inProgress = c.isAnnotationPresent(InProgress.class);
    if (inProgress) {
      out.println("Super is In Progress");
    } else {
      out.println("Super is not In Progress");
    }
  }

  public void testInheritedAnnotation(PrintStream out) throws IOException {
    Class c = Sub.class;
```

Example 6-15. Testing reflection-based annotation methods (continued)

```
    boolean inProgress = c.isAnnotationPresent(InProgress.class);
    if (inProgress) {
      out.println("Sub is In Progress");
    } else {
      out.println("Sub is not In Progress");
    }
  }

  public void testGetAnnotation(PrintStream out)
    throws IOException, NoSuchMethodException {

    Class c = AnnotationTester.class;
    AnnotatedElement element = c.getMethod("calculateInterest",
                                 float.class, float.class);

    GroupTODO groupTodo = element.getAnnotation(GroupTODO.class);
    String assignedTo = groupTodo.assignedTo();

    out.println("TODO Item on Annotation Tester is assigned to: '" +
        assignedTo + "'");
  }

  public void printAnnotations(AnnotatedElement e, PrintStream out)
    throws IOException {

    out.printf("Printing annotations for '%s'%n%n", e.toString());

    Annotation[] annotations = e.getAnnotations();
    for (Annotation a : annotations) {
      out.printf("    * Annotation '%s' found%n",
        a.annotationType().getName());
    }
  }

  public static void main(String[] args) {
    try {
      ReflectionTester tester = new ReflectionTester();

      tester.testAnnotationPresent(System.out);
      tester.testInheritedAnnotation(System.out);

      tester.testGetAnnotation(System.out);

      Class c = AnnotationTester.class;
      AnnotatedElement element = c.getMethod("calculateInterest",
                                   float.class, float.class);
      tester.printAnnotations(element, System.out);
    } catch (Exception e) {
      e.printStackTrace();
    }
  }
}
```

AnnotatedElement is a new interface that the reflection constructs (like Method and Class) implement. It allows access to the new annotation methods used in this code.

What just happened?

The key to much of the code you've just seen is a new interface, java. lang.reflect.AnnotatedElement. In Tiger, the core reflection constructs all implement this interface: Class, Constructor, Field, Method, Package, and AccessibleObject. This allows for the code you've already seen to be introspected for annotations—all these element types provide the following methods as a result of implementing AnnotatedType:

```
public Annotation getAnnotation(Class annotationType);

public Annotation[] getAnnotations();

public Annotation[] getDeclaredAnnotations();

public boolean isAnnotationPresent(Class annotationType);
```

I've simplified the generics syntax for clarity here. If you're into generics, check out the Javadoc on AnnotatedElement for more details on parameters and return types for these methods.

Since any Java program element can be treated as an AnnotatedType, you can always get at an element's annotations using these methods.

What about...

...annotations that aren't marked as visible at runtime? Recall that you have to explicitly set an annotation's retention to RetentionPolicy. RUNTIME for any of this to work. Even if the annotation is retained at compilation (the default behavior), if the VM doesn't load this retention at class-load time, then reflection can't pick up the annotation. In fact, this is why the Inherited and Documented annotations should always be paired up with the following annotation:

```
@Retention(RetentionPolicy.RUNTIME)
```

This ensures that your documentation and/or inheritance is actually readable by code-introspection tools.

TIP

Oddly enough, Deprecation does *not* have runtime retention—it has source retention. So, one of the most valuable annotations, the one indicating deprecation, is undetectable through Java reflection.

The for/in Statement

One of the coolest things about Tiger is that it offers so many new language features. When Java 1.3 and 1.4 were released, they had some new goodies, but most of the changes were either implementation issues (like all the Collection class restructuring), or things you didn't use everyday (like proxies). Tiger is very different, though—you get to write new, funky-looking code, and that's about as good as it gets for hardcore developers.

This chapter examines one of these new language features, the for/in loop. This name is a bit deceiving, as the loop never uses the in keyword; as a result, it's often called *enhanced for*, and even sometimes *foreach*. No matter what you call it, though, it's mostly a convenience function—it doesn't make Java do anything particularly new, but it does save some keystrokes. If you're an emacs or vi guy, that's pretty nice—the less you type, the more advanced a programmer you must be, right?

Ditching Iterators

At its most basic, the for/in statement gets rid of the need to use the java.util.Iterator class. That class, useful in looping over collections of objects, was rarely useful in and of itself. Instead, it made looping, and accessing the objects in that loop, possible. As a means to an end, though, Sun cut out the explicit usage of Iterator and streamlined the basic for loop in the process. As a result, you too can ditch the usage of Iterator.

How do I do that?

You certainly remember the old (yup, it is indeed old now) for loop:

```
/** From ForInTester.java */
public void testForLoop(PrintStream out) throws IOException {
  List list = getList(); // initialize this list elsewhere

  for (Iterator i = list.iterator(); i.hasNext(); ) {
    Object listElement = i.next();
    out.println(listElement.toString());

    // Do something else with this list object
  }
}
```

All the unnamed samples in this chapter are in the class com.oreilly. tiger.ch07. ForInTester. Remember to compile using the "-source 1.5" switch with "javac".

This is a perfect example of Iterator simply being the means of getting at objects in the list, rather than providing real value to the loop. for/in allows this loop to be rewritten:

```
public void testForInLoop(PrintStream out) throws IOException {
  List list = getList(); // initialize this list elsewhere

  for (Object listElement : list) {
    out.println(listElement.toString());

    // Do something else with this list element
  }
}
```

This removal of Iterator has some consequences—see the later labs in the chapter for details.

Notice that the line Object listElement = i.next(); from the first code sample has disappeared. This is the basis of what for/in does—it removes the Iterator from the process.

What just happened?

For those of you into specifications and language structure, the loop is structured like this:

```
for (declaration : expression)
  statement
```

The Java specification defines the precise behavior of the for/in loop by translating it to the equivalent for loops shown below. In these loop translations, the terms *declaration*, *expression*, and *statement* should be replaced with the corresponding part of the for/in loop. The identifiers beginning with # are synthetic variables that the compiler uses for the translation. Their names are not legal Java identifiers, and you cannot use them in the loop body.

A `for/in` loop in which the compile-time type of the expression is `Iterable<E>` (discussed in "Avoiding Unnecessary Typecasts"), is translated to this `for` loop:

```
for ( Iterator<E> #i = (expression).iterator( ); #i.hasNext( ); ) {
    declaration = #i.next( );
    statement
}
```

This sample uses generics, covered in Chapter 2.

If *expression* does not use generics and its compile-time type is just an unparameterized `Iterable`, then the loop is translated in the same way except that the `<E>` is dropped:

```
for ( Iterator #i = (expression).iterator( ); #i.hasNext( ); ) {
    declaration = #i.next( );
    statement
}
```

If the compile-time type of *expression* is an array of type `T[]`, where *T* is any primitive or reference type, then the loop is translated as follows:

```
{
    T[] #a = expression;

    labels

    for (int #i = 0; #i < #a.length; #i++) {
        declaration = #a[ #i ] ;
        statement
    }
}
```

Note that this code is designed to ensure that *expression* is evaluated only once. If the `for/in` loop is labeled with one or more labels, those labels are translated as shown so that they appear after the evaluation of *expression*. This makes a labeled `continue` within the loop statement work correctly.

There are some further points about the syntax of the `for/in` loop that you should be aware of:

- *expression* must be either an array or an object that implements the `java.lang.Iterable` interface. The compiler must be able to ensure this at compile-time—so you can't use a `List` cast to `Object`, for example, and expect things to behave.

- The type of the array or `Iterable` elements must be assignment-compatible with the type of the variable declared in the *declaration*. If the assignment won't work, you're going to get errors.

Using the "final" modifier is a good way to ensure bulletproof code, unless you really need to modify the loop variable.

- The *declaration* usually consists of just a type and a variable name, but it may include a `final` modifier and any appropriate annotations (see Chapter 6 on Annotations). Using `final` prevents the loop variable from taking on any value other than the array or collection element the loop assigns. It also emphasizes the fact that the array or collection cannot be altered through the loop variable.
- The loop variable of the `for/in` loop must be declared as part of the loop, with both a type and a variable name. You cannot use a variable declared outside the loop as you can with the `for` loop.

What about...

...just using a regular for loop? You're welcome to it. `for/in` really doesn't add any functionality—it's ultimately about convenience. And you'll see several instances in this chapter where this convenience comes with a functionality *loss*, rather than gain. So, if you're only in it to get something done, `for/in` doesn't really offer you much, other than the ability to keep up with the number of times you need to iterate over a collection. On the other hand, if your goal in life is to type as little as possible, or if you just want to be the cool guy who uses new and odd-looking structures, `for/in` is perfect.

Iterating over Arrays

`for/in` loops work with two basic types: arrays and collection classes (specifically, only collections that can be iterated over, as detailed in "Making Your Classes Work with for/in"). Arrays are the easiest to iterate over using `for/in`.

How do I do that?

Arrays have their type declared in the initialization statement, as shown here:

```
int[] int_array = new int[4];
String[] args = new String[10];
float[] float_array = new float[20];
```

This means that you can set up your looping variable as that type and just operate upon that variable:

```
public void testArrayLooping(PrintStream out) throws IOException {
    int[] primes = new int[] { 2, 3, 5, 7, 11, 13, 17, 19, 23, 29 };

    // Print the primes out using a for/in loop
    for (int n : primes) {
```

```
    out.println(n);
  }
}
```

This is about as easy as it gets. As a nice benefit, you don't have to worry about the number of times to iterate, and that alone is worth getting to know this loop.

What about...

...iterating over object arrays? No problem at all. Consider the following code:

```java
public void testObjectArrayLooping(PrintStream out) throws IOException {
  List[] list_array = new List[3];

  list_array[0] = getList();
  list_array[1] = getList();
  list_array[2] = getList();

  for (List l : list_array) {
    out.println(l.getClass().getName());
  }
}
```

This code compiles and runs perfectly.

Iterating over Collections

Iterating over a collection works in just about the same way as iterating over an array. The main difference is that you're going to have to add some type-casting, as the objects within a collection aren't compile-time determinable, except when using generics (see the next section on "Avoiding Unnecessary Typecasts" for details on generics and for/in).

How do I do that?

Example 7-1 is a simple program that shows several types of collection iteration.

Example 7-1. Demonstrating the for/in loop with collections

```java
package com.oreilly.tiger.ch07;

import java.util.ArrayList;
import java.util.HashSet;
import java.util.List;
import java.util.Set;

public class ForInDemo {
```

This example is culled from Java in a Nutshell, Fifth Edition (O'Reilly).

Example 7-1. Demonstrating the for/in loop with collections (continued)

```java
public static void main(String[] args) {

    // These are collections we'll iterate over below.
    List wordlist = new ArrayList();
    Set wordset = new HashSet();

    // We start with a basic loop over the elements of an array.
    // The body of the loop is executed once for each element of args[].
    // Each time through one element is assigned to the variable word.
    System.out.println("Assigning arguments to lists...");
    for(String word : args) {
      System.out.print(word + " ");
      wordlist.add(word);
      wordset.add(word);
    }

    System.out.println();

    // Iterate through the elements of the List now.
    // Since lists have an order, these words should appear as above
    System.out.println("Printing words from wordlist " +
      "(ordered, with duplicates)...");
    for(Object word : wordlist) {
      System.out.print((String)word + " ");
    }

    System.out.println();

    // Do the same for the Set. The loop looks the same but by virtue of
    // using a Set, we lose the word order and also discard duplicates.
    System.out.println("Printing words from wordset " +
      "(unordered, no duplicates)...");
    for(Object word : wordset) {
      System.out.print((String)word + " ");
    }
  }
}
```

When compiling this class, you'll get several warnings from the compiler because the code doesn't use a typed list, like List<String>. I'll cover using generics with for/in later in the chapter.

This is pretty basic stuff, so I'll save a tree and cut out repetitive discussion. Here's the output from the program, which should look exactly as expected:

If you're using the build.xml supplied with the examples, just type "ant run-ch07" to see this output.

```
run-ch07:
    [echo] Running Chapter 7 examples from Java 1.5 Tiger: A Developer's
Notebook\n
    [echo] Running ForInDemo...
    [java] Assigning arguments to lists...
    [java] word1 word2 word3 word4 word1
    [java] Printing words from wordlist (ordered, with duplicates)...
    [java] word1 word2 word3 word4 word1
    [java] Printing words from wordset (unordered, no duplicates)...
    [java] word4 word1 word3 word2
```

Avoiding Unnecessary Typecasts

While for/in is nice, you still have to perform all those typecasts, as seen in Example 7-1. If you recall from Chapter 2, though, Tiger introduces some pretty powerful language structures in the form of generics. The main thrust of those new structures is to increase type safety, and that, paired with what you already know about for/in, can increase the convenience of this new loop. You can get away with being specific in your loop iterations, rather than getting an Object from each iteration and then casting that Object to the appropriate type.

How do I do that?

The first step in working with type-specific iterators actually has to occur before you ever type for/in. You need to declare your collections using generics:

```
// These are collections we'll iterate over below.
List<String> wordlist = new ArrayList<String>();
Set<String> wordset = new HashSet<String>();
```

Then write your code normally, except substitute a type-specific variable instead of a generic Object and remove any typecasts:

```
for(String word : wordlist) {
    System.out.print(word + " ");
}
```

Example 7-2 is a generics version of Example 7-1.

Example 7-2. Using the for/in loop with generics

```
package com.oreilly.tiger.ch07;

import java.util.ArrayList;
import java.util.HashSet;
import java.util.List;
import java.util.Set;

public class ForInGenericsDemo {

  public static void main(String[] args) {
```

Example 7-2. Using the for/in loop with generics (continued)

```java
    // These are collections we'll iterate over below.
    List<String> wordlist = new ArrayList<String>();
    Set<String> wordset = new HashSet<String>();

        // We start with a basic loop over the elements of an array.
        // The body of the loop is executed once for each element of args[].
        // Each time through one element is assigned to the variable word.
        System.out.println("Assigning arguments to lists...");
        for(String word : args) {
          System.out.print(word + " ");
          wordlist.add(word);
          wordset.add(word);
        }

        System.out.println();

        // Iterate through the elements of the List now.
        // Since lists have an order, these words should appear as above
        System.out.println("Printing words from wordlist " +
          "(ordered, with duplicates)...");
        for(String word : wordlist) {
          System.out.print(word + " ");
        }

        System.out.println();

        // Do the same for the Set. The loop looks the same but by virtue of
        // using a Set, we lose the word order and also discard duplicates.
        System.out.println("Printing words from wordset " +
          "(unordered, no duplicates)...");
        for(String word : wordset) {
          System.out.print(word + " ");
        }
      }
    }
```

The output is identical to that from Example 7-1 (previously shown in "Iterating over Collections"), so I've omitted it here.

What just happened?

When using generics in this manner, you're essentially offloading all the typecasting (and possible ClassCastExceptions) onto the compiler, rather than dealing with them at runtime. When the collections were declared, the use of generics (<String>, syntactically) allowed the compiler to limit the accepted types passed into the collections. As a nice side effect, your for/in statement can make this same assumption, and since the compiler checks all of this at compile-time, rather than runtimc, your code works, and saves you some typecasting in the process.

Making Your Classes Work with for/in

Despite all the collection options available, there are times when it's still useful to define your own custom objects. In cases where your objects represent some sort of collection, it's a good practice to provide a means of letting other classes iterate over them. In the past, this usually meant ensuring that your class provided a java.util.Iterator, allowing it to work with a for loop. With Tiger, you should consider taking a few extra steps to ensure that your custom objects will work with for/in as well. In addition to working with Iterator, you'll need to learn a new interface, java.lang.Iterable.

How do I do that?

First, familiarize yourself with Example 7-3 and Example 7-4, the Iterator and Iterable interfaces. You'll need to grasp both of these to see how the various loops in Java work.

Note that Iterable is in java.lang, not java.util, as you might expect.

Example 7-3. The Iterator interface

```
package java.util;

public interface Iterator<E> {

  public boolean hasNext();

  public E next();

  public void remove();
}
```

I've obviously stripped this down to the bare essentials; that's all you really need, anyway. These methods should look familiar, although I still find the generics syntax (<E> and E) a bit odd to look at.

Here's Iterable, in the same form:

Example 7-4. The Iterable interface

```
package java.lang;

public interface Iterable<E> {
  public java.util.Iterator<E> iterator();
}
```

There are two basic cases in which Iterator and Iterable become issues when dealing with custom objects:

- Your custom object extends an existing Collection class that already supports for/in.
- Your custom object has to handle iteration manually.

Extending collection classes

The first case is the easiest to deal with, as you can essentially steal behavior from the parent class to do all the work. Example 7-5 shows a simple class that extends List.

Example 7-5. Extending the LinkedList class

```
package com.oreilly.tiger.ch07;

import java.util.LinkedList;
import java.util.List;

public class GuitarManufacturerList extends LinkedList<String> {

  public GuitarManufacturerList() {
    super();
  }

  public boolean add(String manufacturer) {

    if (manufacturer.indexOf("Guitars") == -1) {
      return false;
    } else {
      super.add(manufacturer);
      return true;
    }
  }
}
```

This class doesn't do much in terms of customization—it does require that only String be allowed as a parameter (through the extends LinkedList<String> declaration), and that values passed into the add( ) method have "Guitars" as part of their value. This is a rather hackish way to ensure manufacturers are supplied, but it's useful for an illustration.

You can now use this class as shown in Example 7-6. The example creates a new instance of GuitarManufacturerList, seeds it with some sample data, and then uses for/in to iterate over it. With essentially no work on your part, you get the benefit of iteration from the superclass, LinkedList.

Example 7-6. Iterating over GuitarManufacturerList

```
package com.oreilly.tiger.ch07;

import java.io.IOException;
import java.io.PrintStream;

public class CustomObjectTester {

  /** A custom object that extends List */
  private GuitarManufacturerList manufacturers;

  public CustomObjectTester() {
    this.manufacturers = new GuitarManufacturerList<String>();
  }

  public void testListExtension(PrintStream out) throws IOException {
    // Add some items for good measure
    manufacturers.add("Epiphone Guitars");
    manufacturers.add("Gibson Guitars");

    // Iterate with for/in
    for (String manufacturer : manufacturers) {
      out.println(manufacturer);
    }
  }

  public static void main(String[] args) {
    try {
      CustomObjectTester tester = new CustomObjectTester();

      tester.testListExtension(System.out);
    } catch (Exception e) {
      e.printStackTrace();
    }
  }
}
```

Handling iteration manually

In cases where you're not extending an existing collection class, you've got a little more work to do. Still, you'll usually find yourself borrowing at least *some* behavior from existing collection classes, and avoiding direct implementation of Iterator. Example 7-7 shows a simple text file reader that lists the lines of a file when iterated over.

If you don't pass in "LinkedList <String>" here, and just use "LinkedList", you'll get compiler warnings indicating a possible type mismatch.

Example 7-7. Custom class that doesn't extend a collection

```
package com.oreilly.tiger.ch07;

import java.util.Iterator;
import java.io.BufferedReader;
import java.io.FileReader;
```

Example 7-7. Custom class that doesn't extend a collection (continued)

```java
import java.io.IOException;

/**
 * This class allows line-by-line iteration through a text file.
 * The iterator's remove() method throws UnsupportedOperatorException.
 * The iterator wraps and rethrows IOExceptions as IllegalArgumentExceptions.
 */
public class TextFile implements Iterable<String> {

  // Used by the TextFileIterator class below
  final String filename;

  public TextFile(String filename) {
    this.filename = filename;
  }

  // This is the one method of the Iterable interface
  public Iterator<String> iterator() {
    return new TextFileIterator();
  }


  // This non-static member class is the iterator implementation
  class TextFileIterator implements Iterator<String> {

    // The stream we're reading from
    BufferedReader in;

    // Return value of next call to next()
    String nextline;

    public TextFileIterator() {
      // Open the file and read and remember the first line.
      // We peek ahead like this for the benefit of hasNext().
      try {
        in = new BufferedReader(new FileReader(filename));
        nextline = in.readLine();
      } catch(IOException e) {
        throw new IllegalArgumentException(e);
      }
    }

    // If the next line is non-null, then we have a next line
    public boolean hasNext() {
      return nextline != null;
    }

    // Return the next line, but first read the line that follows it.
    public String next() {
      try {
        String result = nextline;
```

This code sample is from Java in a Nutshell, Fifth Edition (O'Reilly).

Example 7-7. Custom class that doesn't extend a collection (continued)

```java
        // If we haven't reached EOF yet
        if (nextline != null) {
          nextline = in.readLine( ); // Read another line
          if (nextline == null)
            in.close( );              // And close on EOF
        }

        // Return the line we read last time through.
        return result;
      } catch(IOException e) {
        throw new IllegalArgumentException(e);
      }
    }

    // The file is read-only; we don't allow lines to be removed.
    public void remove( ) {
      throw new UnsupportedOperationException( );
    }
  }

  public static void main(String[] args) {
    String filename = "TextFile.java";
    if (args.length > 0)
      filename = args[0];

    for(String line : new TextFile(filename))
      System.out.println(line);
  }
}
```

The interesting work is in the TextFileIterator class, which handles all the work of iteration. The first thing to notice is that this iteration is completely read-only—remove simply throws an UnsupportedOperationException. This is a perfectly legal and useful means of ensuring that programmers understand the use-case your custom classes are designed for. I'll leave you to work through the rest of the details; the source code is pretty self-explanatory.

Determining List Position and Variable Value

for/in, more than anything else, is about convenience. However, with that convenience comes a degree of lost flexibility. One such example is the inability to determine the position in a list that the for/in construct resides at. As your code executes within the for/in loop, there is no way to access the position in the list. Additionally, the list variable itself isn't accessible, making its access equally impossible.

How do I do that?

In short, you don't. Sometimes it's just as important to realize what you *can't* do as it is to learn what you *can*.

A common iteration technique is to use the loop variable, especially if it's numerical, in the loop body itself:

```
List<String> wordList = new LinkedList<String>();
for (int i=0; i<args.length; i++) {
  wordList.add("word " + (i+1) + ": '" + args[i] + "'");
}
```

This is perfectly legitimate, and really useful if you're performing some sort of count. However, it's impossible to access the iterator in a for/in loop, as that's kept internal (and not even generated until compilation takes place). In this case, you're out of luck. You can use for/in to display the results of a situation like this, but not to make the assignment itself:

```
public void determineListPosition(PrintStream out, String[] args)
   throws IOException {

List<String> wordList = new LinkedList<String>();

   for (int i=0; i<args.length; i++) {
    wordList.add("word " + (i+1) + ": '" + args[i] + "'");
  }

   for (String word : wordList) {
    out.println(word);
  }
}
```

This is hardly a severe limitation, but it's one you should be aware of.

Another common usage of lists is `String` concatenation, and that illustrates another of the for/in limitations. It's common in `String` concatenation to add separators between all but the last of a set of words, such as when printing a list. This separator is often a comma or perhaps a space:

```
StringBuffer longList = new StringBuffer();
for (int i = 0, len=wordList.size(); i < len; i++) {
  if (i < (len-1)) {
    longList.append(wordList.get(i))
           .append(", ");
  } else {
    longList.append(wordList.get(i));
  }
}
out.println(longList);
```

Chapter 7: The for/in Statement

Here, all but the last word in the list has a comma appended to it, while the last one is appended without a comma. This makes for a nice list output. However, this rather simple task is impossible with for/in, because the variable that is used to do all the work, i, is inaccessible in a for/in loop. Again, a fairly minor inconvenience, but it's certainly not time to retire our old friend for just yet.

Removing List Items in a for/in Loop

Another common task in loop iteration, particularly over collections, is in-loop modification. This is all done through the iterator, as directly modifying the collection creates all sorts of nasty loop problems. Instead, using methods such as remove( ) from java.util.Iterator allows modifications in a loop-safe way. However, since the iterator is hidden in for/in, this is another limitation of for/in.

How do I do that?

This is another one of those "You can't" recipes. To see exactly what it is you *can't* do, take a look at the following code:

```
public void removeListItems(PrintStream out, String[] args)
  throws IOException {

  List<String> wordList = new LinkedList<String>();

  // Assign some words
  for (int i=0; i<args.length; i++) {
    wordList.add("word " + (i+1) + ": '" + args[i] + "'");
  }

  // Remove all words with "1" in them. Impossible with for/in
  for (Iterator i = wordList.iterator(); i.hasNext(); ) {
    String word = (String)i.next();
    if (word.indexOf("1") != -1) {
      i.remove();
    }
  }

  // You can print the words using for/in
  for (String word : wordList) {
    out.println(word);
  }
}
```

In particular, notice the second for loop, which uses remove( ) to yank any words in the List with "1" in the text. This depends on the usage of Iterator, which isn't available in for/in, so you're out of luck here.

What about...

...anything else that involves knowing where you are in the list? Nope— it's not possible. Here are just a few examples of other things you *can't* do with for/in:

- Iterate backward through the elements of an array or List.
- Use a single loop counter to access similarly numbered or positioned elements in two distinct arrays or collections.
- Iterate through the elements of a List using calls to get( ) rather than calls to its iterator.

Watch out for this last one—it is a legitimate performance concern. For the java.util.ArrayList class, for example, looping with the size( ) and get( ) methods is measurably faster than using the list's Iterator. In many cases, the performance difference is negligible and irrelevant. But, when writing an inner loop or other performance-critical code, you might prefer to use a for loop with the get( ) method instead of a for/in loop.

CHAPTER 8

Static Imports

All right, let's begin with a fair warning—this isn't a very sexy chapter. It's not as exciting as generics, it's not as (obviously) missing a feature in the language as varargs, it's not even as cool as the for/in loop. Instead, this chapter is about a feature that is completely convenience-based. It adds no new functionality to the language, and it doesn't even have much to do with how you write code. Sort of an inauspicious beginning, huh?

Still, that said, static imports are extremely cool, especially when you start to pile on additional language features, such as enumerated types. In a nutshell, static imports allow you to import static classes, variables, and enums, and reference them easily in your code. While you may not get any new functionality, the convenience here is very, very nice. As I've said before, I don't know any good programmer who just loves typing out really long variable names, ten or fifteen times in their programs. Static imports help with just that task, and, as such, are very much worth covering.

Importing Static Members

If you've ever done any output in Java, you've typed System.out at least a few times. While there are lots of better ways to handle output, there is perhaps none as simple, direct, and to-the-point as good old System.out.println() and System.err.println(). However, it's annoying to type System.out and System.err time and time again (at least, it is for me). In Tiger, this annoyance is gone, via static imports.

If you try and import something non-static with this syntax, all you get is a "cannot find symbol" compiler error—it's not very descriptive.

How do I do that?

Anytime you have a static member, like `out` and `err` in the `java.lang.System` class, you can import those static members into your code:

```
import static java.lang.System.err;
import static java.lang.System.out;
```

You just use `import static` instead of `import`. Magically, your code can now use the methods of these static members without prefacing those methods with the static member's package name, as seen in Example 8-1.

Example 8-1. Using statically imported member variables

```
package com.oreilly.tiger.ch08;

import static java.lang.System.err;
import static java.lang.System.out;

public class StaticImporter {

  public static void main(String[] args) {
    if (args.length < 2) {
      err.println(
        "Incorrect usage: java com.oreilly.tiger.ch08 [arg1] [arg2]");
      return;
    }

    out.println("Good morning, " + args[0]);
    out.println("Have a " + args[1] + " day!");
  }
}
```

As said before, this isn't anything particularly revolutionary, but it's certainly a nice bonus to the language.

Note that Arrays.sort( ) is a heavily overloaded method. This import directive imports the method by its name, and not any particular overloading of it.

As an added bonus, this same thing applies to static methods, in addition to static variables. For example, consider the `java.util.Arrays` class, which has several static methods, such as `binarySearch( )`, `sort( )`, and `equals( )`. These methods are just static members of the class, and can be imported, just like the `err` and `out` members in Example 8-1:

```
import static java.util.Arrays.sort;
```

You can now just code as shown here:

```
sort(myObjectArray);  // no need to use Arrays.sort( )
```

This is a particularly nice improvement to the language, I think.

What about...

...static member types? A *member type* is a type defined within another class. For example, the java.lang.Character class defines a class within its body, called Subset. The formal name of this class, because it does not stand on its own, is Character.Subset (and it appears that way within the JavaDocs). You can import a member type, in Tiger and in previous versions, with a normal import statement:

```
import java.lang.Character.Subset;
```

This is a little-known, little-used feature of Java that has nothing to do with Tiger. However, where Tiger does come in is adding the ability to do static imports. In the case of Character.Subset, not only is Subset a member type, it's a *static* member type—meaning that it could also be imported as seen here:

Anonymous inner classes defined within a method are not members, and cannot be imported.

```
import static java.lang.Character.Subset;
```

So, which is correct? Actually, both. However, you shouldn't have both in the same code—just one or the other. Otherwise, compilers will gripe about a name conflict (two identically named types). Personally, I like the clarity of import static for this sort of thing, as it reminds me that Character.Subset is static—but that's style more than any real best practice.

Using Wildcards in Static Imports

While importing a single member is a nice addition, there are times when you may want to import a lot of members. In these cases, you could easily fill a page with all the import static declarations you'd need. Luckily, wildcards work perfectly well with static imports.

How do I do that?

Piece of cake...just use a wildcard, as you would with normal import statements:

```
import static java.lang.Math.*;
```

Now you can use expressions like the following in your code:

```
float foo = sqrt(abs(sin(bar)));
```

Again, nothing flashy here, but well worth knowing. It's possible to import anything declared as static into the Java namespace. However, you couldn't do something like this:

```
import static java.lang.System.out.println;
```

That's because while out is static, the method println( ) is not. Be careful to keep your static and non-static items straight.

What about...

...all the code legibility lost by doing this sort of thing? It's certainly possible to go crazy with imports, and lose all track of which methods belong to which class. Of course, this comes from someone who almost never uses wildcards in *normal* import statements:

```
import java.io.IOException;
import java.io.PrintWriter;
import javax.servlet.ServletException;
import javax.servlet.GenericServlet;
// etc.
```

Personally, I like it to be obvious what classes are used, as opposed to dropping an import java.io.* statement into code. But that's a stylistic decision, not a functional one, and now Tiger lets you keep whatever preference you choose.

As a best practice, though, I'd recommend you only use static imports if you were going to use a static member more than three times. In other words, there's value in the clarity of code that reads Math.sqrt( ) as opposed to just sqrt( ), when that method is only used once in the entire program. However, if you're using the method fifty times, then it's just as clear to add a static import for the method and then use it without the prefix.

Importing Enumerated Type Values

The next natural thought in working with static imports is to use them in conjunction with another Tiger feature, enumerated values (detailed in Chapter 3). Since the compiler declares enumerated values as public, static, and final, they are great candidates for being statically imported.

How do I do that?

Remember that enums are just a specialized type of Java class. As a result, the syntax to use them is no different than what you've already seen. Example 8-2 imports the Grade values from Chapter 3, and then uses them in a simple program.

Example 8-2. Importing enum values

```java
package com.oreilly.tiger.ch08;

import static java.lang.System.out;
import static com.oreilly.tiger.ch03.Grade.*;

import java.io.IOException;
import java.io.PrintStream;
import com.oreilly.tiger.ch03.Student;

public class EnumImporter {

  private Student[] students = new Student[4];

  public EnumImporter() {
    students[0] = new Student("Brett", "McLaughlin");
    students[0].assignGrade(A);

    students[1] = new Student("Leigh", "McLaughlin");
    students[0].assignGrade(B);

    students[2] = new Student("Dean", "McLaughlin");
    students[0].assignGrade(C);

    students[3] = new Student("Robbie", "McLaughlin");
    students[0].assignGrade(INCOMPLETE);
  }

  public void printGrades(PrintStream out) throws IOException {
    for (Student student : students) {
      if ((student.getGrade() == INCOMPLETE) ||
          (student.getGrade() == D)) {
        // Make this student retake this class
      }
    }
  }

  public static void main(String[] args) {
    try {
      EnumImporter importer = new EnumImporter();

      importer.printGrades(out);
    } catch (Exception e) {
      e.printStackTrace();
    }
  }
}
```

Dean and Robbie appear to be spending too much time playing guitar and banjo, and not enough time studying!

Nowhere in this class do you see Grade.A or Grade.INCOMPLETE, which really reduces the overall clutter. As a result, the code is a good deal clearer, and even a little shorter (not a bad thing).

This same trick works for enums that are declared inline within a class; remember the Downloader example from Chapter 3? It's reprinted here for convenience:

```
package com.oreilly.tiger.ch03;

public class Downloader {

  public enum DownloadStatus { INITIALIZING, IN_PROGRESS, COMPLETE };

  // Class body

}
```

You can import these into another class with the following line:

```
import static com.oreilly.tiger.ch03.Downloader.DownloadStatus.*;
```

As I mentioned back in Chapter 3, though, this is more of a hack than a real programming solution. If you need an enum in more than one class, it's a better practice to define the enum separately (in it's own *.java* file), and then use it in both classes, rather than tying its declaration into a particular class file.

Importing Multiple Members with the Same Name

When you start digging into the rules for Java imports and the Java namespace (the names available to a piece of code, with or without package prefixes), things begin to get a little hairy. For example, it is illegal to have two type names that are identical within the same package. By extension, you can't import two types into your code with the same name.

On the other hand, this is precisely the sort of thing you *want* when dealing with methods—it's called overloading. So you may have three, four, or more methods of the same name, all taking different parameters, and javac will happily compile your code. So here's the short version—types must be named uniquely, methods need not be. And if you think overloading was cool in previous versions of Java, wait until you see the implications for Tiger!

How do I do that?

Suppose you import the sort( ) method from the java.util.Arrays class:

```
import static java.util.Arrays.sort;
```

There are 18 different versions of this method, and you get all of them via overloading. However, let's also assume that you also need the Collections.sort() methods as well (there are two versions of that one). Since this method takes different sets of arguments than any of the 18 versions you've already imported into your namespace, just add another import statement:

```
import static java.util.Arrays.sort;
import static java.util.Collections.sort;
```

Just like that, you're all set, and you get even more overloading. Now the compiler will actually decide, based on your arguments, which method, and even which class, to use to process your method call. Pretty cool!

What about...

...naming conflicts? As already stated, you'll get a compiler error if you import two types with the same name into your program. So the following lines would be illegal in a source listing:

```
import java.util.Arrays;
import com.oreilly.tiger.ch08.Arrays;
```

You'd get the following error:

```
[javac]   src\ch08\SortImporter.java:4:
              java.util.Arrays is already defined in a single-type import
[javac] import com.oreilly.tiger.ch08.Arrays;
[javac] ^
```

When it comes to naming conflicts among imported static methods, though, things are a little more obscure. I've created a simple class, shown in Example 8-3, that defines a method of sort() with the exact same arguments as one of the sort() methods in java.util.Arrays.

Example 8-3. Setting up a namespace conflict

```
package com.oreilly.tiger.ch08;

public class Arrays {

  public static void sort(float[] a) {
    // Do nothing
    // This is just used to illustrate some naming conflicts
  }

}
```

As cool as this is, it really increases the work that someone on the debugging or testing team has to do to figure out what's going on in your code.

Now, add you can create a naming conflict with the following lines in another class:

```
import static java.util.Arrays.sort;
import static java.util.Collections.sort;
import static com.oreilly.tiger.ch08.Arrays.sort;
```

In theory, there is only a potential conflict here—but both java.util. Arrays and the new Arrays class define a method with the same name (sort), that takes an identical argument set (float[]). However, the compiler will not choke on this—in fact, it doesn't even provide you a warning! As best I can tell, you're being given the benefit of the doubt as a programmer (never a good thing!). However, if you try and use the method that's a problem, things go wrong, as shown in the following code:

```
public static void main(String[] args) {
  float[] f = new float[] {5, 4, 6, 3, 2, 1};

  sort(f);
}
```

This will cause a compiler error:

```
[javac] src\ch08\SortImporter.java:16: reference to sort is ambiguous,
         both method sort(float[]) in com.oreilly.tiger.ch08.Arrays and
           method sort(float[]) in java.util.Arrays match
[javac]     sort(f);
[javac]     ^
```

So namespaces are a little tricky, and you'd do well to be careful when importing static members of the same name from multiple classes.

Shadowing Static Imports

As a final act of complete confusion in your code, you're welcome to *shadow* your imports, static or otherwise. Shadowing is the process of having a member variable (or field, or method) effectively hide something that is already in the Java namespace through an import.

How do I do that?

Simply declare a member variable named the same as what is imported, and that you want to shadow. Example 8-4 is an example of just that process in action.

Example 8-4. Shadowing an import

```
package com.oreilly.tiger.ch08;

import static java.lang.System.err;
import static java.lang.System.out;

import java.io.IOException;
import java.io.PrintStream;

public class StaticImporter {

  public static void writeError(PrintStream err, String msg)
    throws IOException {

    // Note that err in the parameter list overshadows the imported err
    err.println(msg);
  }

  public static void main(String[] args) {
    if (args.length < 2) {
      err.println(
        "Incorrect usage: java com.oreilly.tiger.ch08 [arg1] [arg2]");
      return;
    }

    out.println("Good morning, " + args[0]);
    out.println("Have a " + args[1] + " day!");

    try {
      writeError(System.out, "Error occurred.");
    } catch (IOException e) {
      e.printStackTrace();
    }
  }
}
```

Example 8-4 is an updated version of Example 8-1.

Note that a variable named err is defined, local to the writeError() method. That variable, in that method, will shadow the err variable imported from java.lang.System. Keep in mind, though, that this adds yet another layer of obfuscation to your code. It's almost always easier to just rename your variable to avoid this type of confusion, and save everyone some headaches:

```
public static void writeError(PrintStream errorStream, String msg)
  throws IOException {

  errorStream.println(msg);
}
```

Formatting

Tiger has a rather innocent looking new class called java.util. Formatter. Despite its looks, though, this one class provides new functionality to all of Tiger's output methods. To cut to the chase, all you former C programmers will finally get to compile code with printf( ) in it—there, now aren't you smiling already?

Creating a Formatter

The simplest way to get started with the Formatter class is to create a new instance of it, and then do some work. You'll see in later labs that this isn't always the *best* way to go about business, but it's as good a starting point as any.

How do I do that?

Formatter has several constructors, listed here:

```
// No-args version -- not particularly useful
public Formatter();

// Basically, the no-args version with a locale
public Formatter(Locale l);

// Creates a formatter with the supplied destination (sink)
public Formatter(Appendable a);

// Creates a formatter with the destination, using the supplied locale
public Formatter(Appendable a, Locale l);

// Creates a new formatter with the filename as the sink
public Formatter(String fileName);
```

```
// Creates a new formatter with a file as the sink, using the specified
charset
public Formatter(String fileName, String csn);

// Same as above, but with a locale
public Formatter(String fileName, String csn, Locale l);
```

This is a pretty wide range of options, and should cover your most basic formatting needs. Thus, you could use code such as this to create a Formatter targeted at a StringBuilder:

```
StringBuilder sb = new StringBuilder();
Formatter formatter = new Formatter(sb, Locale.FRANCE);

// The next lab details what you can do with Formatter
```

I realize this seems sort of trivial, but it's meant to be. Formatter is a new class, but not a particularly difficult one to master.

If you're unfamiliar with StringBuilder, check out the lab at the end of this chapter.

Writing Formatted Output

Once you've got your Formatter instance, I'm going to make the rather silly leap to assuming you want to use it. The best way to do this is through the format() method.

How do I do that?

First, let's deal with the easy stuff—this new class has some simple methods to let you find out how it's configured:

```
// Return the locale for this Formatter
public Locale locale();

// Returns the last thrown IOException by the sink
public IOException ioException();

// Returns the sink for output
public Appendable out();
```

There is also a close() method, which, unsurprisingly, closes the formatter when you're done with output (which is particularly important when you're holding onto file resources).

A sink is a term used to refer to where output goes to—sort of a collection bin. Often this is some output mechanism, like an Output-Stream, or an object that can later output what is in the sink, such as StringBuffer.

The most interesting methods are the two versions of format():

```
// Notice the varargs for multiple object arguments
public Formatter format(String format, Object... args);

// Same as above, but with a Locale
public Formatter format(Locale l, String format, Object... args);
```

While these methods return the object they're working on, it's common to not assign this return value, and merely discard it instead. This method works, as shown here (in a simple example):

```
StringBuilder sb = new StringBuilder();
Formatter formatter = new Formatter(sb);

formatter.format("Remaining account balance: $%.2f", balance);
```

If you're unclear on how varargs or the Object... notation works, check out Chapter 5.

This example would output the value in the balance variable, as a floating point number, with two decimal places allowed. For those of you used to methods like printf() in C, this is no big deal. For those of you who didn't grow up on a steady diet of structs, this is still probably a bit odd.

First, the String to output is passed in—no big deal here. However, within that String are several items that are dynamic—not known until run-time. In the previous example, the dynamic item is the value of balance. Anytime you need to insert dynamic data like that, the % indicates that a value will be supplied, in the argument list (remember Object...), to be inserted into the String. The characters *after* the % indicate how that value should be formatted:

```
%[argument][flags][width][.precision]type
```

Types

The only requirement here is *type*, so the example you saw previously could be written in its simplest format as shown here:

```
formatter.format("Remaining account balance: $%f", balance);
```

Table 9-1 is a rundown of all the available types. Note that these are actually *conversion types*—if the value supplied is not in the specified format, a conversion is attempted.

If uppercase and lowercase versions are listed (%s, %S), the uppercase variant produces the same output as the lowercase variant, except that all lowercase letters are converted to uppercase.

Table 9-1. Formatter conversion types

Conversion symbol	Description
%%	Escape sequence to allow printing of % in a String.
%a, %A	Formats the value as a floating-point number in exponential notation, using base-16 for the decimal part, and base-10 for the exponent part. Arguments must be Float, Double, or BigDecimal.
%b, %B	Formats the value as either "true" or "false" (or "TRUE" or "FALSE", for %B). For boolean values, this works as expected. For all other values, any non-null value is "true", while null values are "false".

Table 9-1. Formatter conversion types (continued)

Conversion symbol	Description
%c, %C	Formats the value supplied as a single character. Supplied value must be a Byte, Short, Character, or Integer.
%d	Formats the value as a base-10 integer. Arguments must be Byte, Short, Integer, Long, or BigInteger.
%e, %E	Formats the value as a base-10 floating-point number, using exponential notation. Arguments must be Float, Double, or BigDecimal.
%f	Formats the value as a floating-point number in base-10, *without* exponential notation. Arguments must be Float, Double, or BigDecimal.
%g, %G	Formats the value as a base-10 floating point number, with no more than 6 significant digits (if *precision* is not supplied). Arguments must be Float, Double, or BigDecimal.
%h, %H	Formats the value as a hexadecimal representation of the value's hashcode.
%n	Outputs the line separator for the platform.
%o	Formats the value as a base-8 octal integer. Arguments must be Byte, Short, Integer, Long, or BigInteger.
%s, %S	Formats the value supplied as a String, usually through calling toString( ) on the object.
%t, %T	The prefix for *all* date/time conversions. All date/time types (listed in Table 9-2) requires a Date, Calendar, or Long argument. Note that the t or T determines uppercase/lowercase, rather than the case of the letter *following* the t/T.
%x, %X	Formats the value as a base-16 hexadecimal integer. Arguments must be Byte, Short, Integer, Long, or BigInteger.

Because date/time are a bit of a special case, they are listed in their own table, Table 9-2.

Table 9-2. Date and time conversion types

Conversion symbol	Description
%tA	The locale-specific full name of the day of the week
%ta	The locale-specific abbreviation of the day of the week
%tB	The locale-specific full name of the month
%tb	The locale-specific abbreviation for the month
%tC	The century, from 00 to 99 (by dividing by 100)
%tc	The complete date and time
%tD	The date in short numeric form
%td	The day of the month, as a two-digit number—01 to 31

Table 9-2. Date and time conversion types (continued)

Conversion symbol	Description
%tE	The date as milliseconds since midnight, UTC, on Jan. 1st, 1970
%te	The day of the month, without leading zeroes—1 to 31
%tF	The numeric day in ISO8601 format
%tH	Two-digit hour of the day, using a 24-hour clock—00 to 23
%th	The abbreviated month name (identical to %tb)
%tI	Two-digit hour of the day using a 12-hour clock—01 to 12
%tj	Three digit day of the year—001 to 366
%tk	Hour of the day on a 24-hour clock—0 to 23
%tL	Three-digit milliseconds within the second—000 to 999
%tl	Hour of the day on a 12-hour clock—1 to 12
%tM	Two-digit minute within the hour—00 to 59
%tm	Two-digit month of the year—01 to 12 (01 to 13 for lunar calendars)
%tN	Nanosecond within the second, expressed as nine digits
%tp	Locale-specific morning or afternoon indicator
%tR	The hour and minute on a 24-hour clock
%tr	The hour, minute, and second on a 24-hour clock
%tS	Two-digit seconds within the minute—00 to 59
%ts	Seconds since the beginning of the epoch
%tT	Time in hours, minutes, and seconds, using a 24-hour format
%tY	Four-digit (at least) year
%ty	Last two digits of the year—00 to 99
%tZ	Abbreviation for the timezone
%tZ	The timezone as a numeric offset from GMT

I know that's a lot of dry detail, especially for a down-and-dirty book such as this, but now you've got all the conversion codes at your fingertips.

Precision

You can add an optional precision indicator to your format string:

```
formatter.format("Remaining account balance: $%.2f", balance);
```

By adding .2, it indicates that the value of balance should be given two decimal places of precision, ensuring you get a number like 2510.00 instead of 2510. .2 in this case fills the *precision* spot in the syntax list. Here are a few rules that apply:

- For %e, %E, and %f, the default precision is 6.
- For %g and %G, the precision is the *total* number of significant digits to be displayed.
- For %s, %h, and %b (and their uppercase variants), the precision determines the maximum characters output.

WARNING

If the formatted output exceeds *precision*, the output is truncated. Additionally, specifying precision for other conversion types can result in an exception at runtime (not compile time).

- Trailing zeros are always added as needed, to match the specified (or default) precision, for numeric types.

Width

In addition to precision, the total minimum number of characters to be produced can be set through *width*:

```
formatter.format("Remaining account balance: $%6.2f", balance);
```

Here, the balance will be shown with *at least* six digits of total characters. If the formatted output is less than the specified width, zeroes are added as padding on the left (values are right-justified). A width can be specified for any conversion type other than %n (which isn't a true conversion type anyway—it's a line separator).

TIP

If *precision* is smaller than *width*, the formatted value is truncated to the supplied precision, and then padded with zeros to the supplied width.

Argument

By default, calls to format( ) (and printf( ), detailed in "Using the printf( ) Convenience Method") match each conversion with the arguments supplied to the method, in order, one after another. However, you can optionally change that behavior with an argument indicator:

```
formatter.format("Remaining account balance: $%6.2f"+
            "(Today's total balance:    $%<8.2f)", balance);
```

Here, the < argument is used to indicate that the previous argument should be used (again), rather than continuing on. This is a clever way to reuse arguments without listing them in the argument list multiple times. It also allows the same argument to be formatted in different ways:

```
formatter.format("Date: %tD%nTime: %<tr%n", System.currentTimeMillis());
```

You can also explicitly refer to an argument by its position, using the syntax [arg-number]$. Thus, you could refer to the second argument in the list with %2$.

Flags

The final option you have is to specify one or more flags, which are non-numeric characters that appear just before width and precision indicators:

```
formatter.format("Remaining account balance: $%(,6.2f"+
              "(Today's total balance:     $%(,<8.2f)", balance);
```

In this example, two flags are used: the parenthetical (((), and the comma indicator (,). The parenthetical indicates that negative values should be placed in parentheses, and the comma instructs the formatter to insert commas (or any other local-specific grouping separator) between digits. So, output from these instructions would look like $(8,134.28), or $(008,134.28), depending on the width specified. Table 9-3 has the complete list of valid flags.

Table 9-3. Format flags

Flag	Description
-	Indicates that the formatted value should be left-justified, based on *width*.
#	Indicates that the formatted output should appear in *alternate form*. For %o, this means a leading 0. For %x and %X, output will include a leading 0x (0X). For %s and %S, the flag is passed on to the object's formatTo( ) method.
+	Indicates that numeric output should always include a sign (+ or -).
' '	The space value (which is hard to show in a book) indicates that non-negative values should be prefixed with a space. This is generally used for alignment with negative numbers.
(	Indicates that negative numbers should appear in parentheses.
0	Indicates that numeric values should be padded on the left.
,	Indicates that the locale-specific grouping character should be used for numeric values.

The # flag only works in conjunction with %s and %S if the argument implements java.util. Formattable.

Output

It's worth saying that with all of this talk of formatting, nothing is output until you actually *use* your sink:

```
System.out.println(sb.toString());
```

It's easy to do lots of great formatting work, and then forget to actually output the results. There are also several other ways to output formatted strings like this, covered in the following recipes.

If you've chosen a stream as your sink, then the output occurs as you format it.

Using the format( ) Convenience Method

The Formatter object is a nice addition to the language—however, it's a bit inconvenient to break your program flow for four or five statements related only to formatting, and then get back to the job at hand. It's even more distracting when you have to do this five or six times in a single code block. Fortunately, there are some nice convenience methods that make these steps largely unnecessary.

How do I do that?

The classes java.io.PrintStream, java.io.PrintWriter, and java.lang. String all have a new method available to them in Tiger, called format( ). All three classes have two versions of the method:

```
public [returnType] format(String format, Object... args);
public [returnType] format(Locale l, String format, Object... args);
```

TIP

The String versions of these methods are static.

This should look awfully familiar if you just read "Writing Formatted Output". For each of these, *returnType* is the object type itself (so a PrintStream, PrintWriter, or String). For both PrintStream and PrintWriter, the output is usually ignored; for String, the method is usually invoked statically and the result is assigned to a new String. Each method used varargs, as did the Formatter object, allowing you to pass in as many arguments to be used by the format string as needed.

So, rather than having to create a new Formatter, set one of these objects as its sink, and format it, you can handle all of this in a single step:

```
String balanceStmt =
  String.format("Remaining account balance: $%(,6.2f"+
                "(Today's total balance:     $%(,<8.2f)", balance);
```

This saves a few steps, and now the balanceStmt String can be output easily. This method is even more useful for the stream and writer versions:

```
System.out.format("Date: %tD%nTime: %<tr%n", System.currentTimeMillis());
```

Using the printf( ) Convenience Method

For those of you who are die-hard C and C++ fans, Tiger gives you the ability to type printf( ) once more.

How do I do that?

In "Using the format( ) Convenience Method," you saw how both the PrintStream and PrintWriter classes offer a new method called format( ) to handle formatted output. Each class also has a method called printf( ), which does *exactly the same thing*. That's right— printf( ) and format( ) are interchangeable. So, if you favor using printf( ) over format( ), you're free to do so, as Example 9-1 shows.

Example 9-1. Using printf( ) instead of format( )

```
package com.oreilly.tiger.ch09;

import java.io.BufferedReader;
import java.io.File;
import java.io.FileReader;

public class FormatTester {

  public static void main(String[] args) {
    String filename = args[0];

    try {
      File file = new File(filename);
      FileReader fileReader = new FileReader(file);
      BufferedReader reader = new BufferedReader(fileReader);
```

Example 9-1. Using printf( ) instead of format( ) (continued)

```
    String line;
    int i = 1;
    while ((line = reader.readLine()) != null) {
      System.out.printf("Line %d: %s%n", i++, line);
    }

  } catch (Exception e) {
    System.err.printf("Unable to open file named '%s': %s",
                  filename, e.getMessage());
  }
 }
}
```

Threading

From its earliest days, Java has been a multithreaded environment. While the threading capabilities are formidable in Java 1.4, Tiger introduces a whole new slew of concurrency utilities, allowing for further tweaking of your multithreaded programs.

Handling Uncaught Exceptions in Threads

Normally a Java thread (represented by any class that extends java. lang.Thread) stops when its run( ) method completes. In an abnormal case, such as when something goes wrong, the thread can terminate by throwing an exception. This exception trickles up the thread's ThreadGroup hierarchy, and if it gets to the root ThreadGroup, the default behavior is to print out the thread's name, exception name, exception message, and exception stack trace.

To get around this behavior (at least in Java 1.4 and earlier), you've got to insert your own code into the ThreadGroup hierarchy, handle the exception, and prevent delegation back to the root ThreadGroup. While this is certainly possible, you'll have to define your own subclass of ThreadGroup, make sure any Threads you create are assigned to that group, and generally do a lot of coding that has very little to do with the task at hand—actually handling the uncaught exception. Tiger simplifies all this dramatically, and lets you define uncaught exception handling on a per-Thread basis.

How do I do that?

The java.lang.Thread class defines a nested interface in Tiger, called Thread.UncaughtExceptionHandler. You can create your own implementation of this interface and pass it to your target Thread's setUncaughtExceptionHandler( ) method (also new in Tiger). Example 10-1 is a simple Thread that does just this.

Example 10-1. Thread with uncaught exception handler

```java
package com.oreilly.tiger.ch10;

public class BubbleSortThread extends Thread {

  private int[] numbers;

  public BubbleSortThread(int[] numbers) {
    setName("Simple Thread");
    setUncaughtExceptionHandler(
      new SimpleThreadExceptionHandler( ));
    this.numbers = numbers;
  }

  public void run( ) {
    int index = numbers.length;
    boolean finished = false;
    while (!finished) {
      index--;
      finished = true;
      for (int i=0; i<index; i++) {
        // Create error condition
        if (numbers[i+1] < 0) {
          throw new IllegalArgumentException(
            "Cannot pass negative numbers into this thread!");
        }

        if (numbers[i] > numbers[i+1]) {
          // swap
          int temp = numbers[i];
          numbers[i] = numbers[i+1];
          numbers[i+1] = temp;

          finished = false;
        }
      }
    }
  }
}

class SimpleThreadExceptionHandler implements
    Thread.UncaughtExceptionHandler {
```

I used a bubble sort for the example, but you should know that sorts like quicksort are much faster (and therefore much cooler).

Example 10-1. Thread with uncaught exception handler (continued)

```
public void uncaughtException(Thread t, Throwable e) {
    System.err.printf("%s: %s at line %d of %s%n",
        t.getName(),
        e.toString(),
        e.getStackTrace()[0].getLineNumber(),
        e.getStackTrace()[0].getFileName());
  }
}
```

This is a pretty normal Thread, with the exception of two items. First, there is a rather odd condition thrown into the sorting algorithm: if an int less than zero is in the supplied array, an IllegalArgumentException is tossed out. Second, to handle this (rather odd) case, an implementation of Thread.UncaughtExceptionHandler is defined, which prints out some additional information about the problem, including a line number and filename.

To see this in action, you can use Example 10-2, a simple test program.

Example 10-2. Testing the uncaught exception handler

```
package com.oreilly.tiger.ch10;

import java.io.IOException;
import java.io.PrintStream;

public class ThreadTester {

  private int[] posArray = new int[] {1, 3, 6, 3, 4, 2, 5};
  private int[] negArray = new int[] {-2, -8, -3, -9, -10};

  public ThreadTester() {
  }

  public void testBubbleSort(PrintStream out) throws IOException {
    Thread t1 = new BubbleSortThread(posArray);
    t1.start();

    out.println("Testing with postive numbers...");
    // Wait for the thread to complete
    try {
      t1.join();
      printArray(posArray, out);
    } catch (InterruptedException ignored) { }

    Thread t2 = new BubbleSortThread(negArray);
    t2.start();

    out.println("Testing with negative numbers...");
    try {
```

Example 10-2. Testing the uncaught exception handler (continued)

```
    t2.join();
    printArray(negArray, out);
  } catch (InterruptedException ignored) { }
}

private void printArray(int[] a, PrintStream out) throws IOException {
  for (int n : a) {
    out.println(n);
  }
  out.println();
}

public static void main(String[] args) {
  ThreadTester tester = new ThreadTester();

  try {
    tester.testBubbleSort(System.out);
  } catch (Exception e) {
    e.printStackTrace();
  }
}

}
```

Running "ant run-ch10" will automate this for you.

If you run this example, which generates an error when negative numbers are supplied in negArray, you'll see the SimpleExceptionHandler in action:

```
[echo] Running ThreadTester...
[java] Testing with postive numbers...
[java] 1
[java] 2
[java] 3
[java] 3
[java] 4
[java] 5
[java] 6

[java] Testing with negative numbers...
[java] Simple Thread: java.lang.IllegalArgumentException: Cannot pass
       negative numbers into this thread! at line 23 of
       BubbleSortThread.java
[java] -2
[java] -8
[java] -3
[java] -9
[java] -10
```

While this is a fine example, it's still a bad idea to write to the console, or even System.err, unless you're sure where those errors are going, and that they will be seen by some set of human eyes. A better idea would be to log these errors somewhere useful.

Also, notice that the negative array (negArray) doesn't get sorted. That's because the thread threw an exception and never completed the sort.

What about...

...setting an UncaughtExceptionHandler for all threads? Install a default handler: pass an implementation of Thread.UncaughtExceptionHandler to the Thread.setDefaultUncaughtExceptionHandler( ), which is, of course, a static method:

```
Thread.setUncaughtExceptionHandler(new MyDefaultHandler( ));
```

If a Thread has its own handler, that of course overrides the default handler. In fact, here's the exact sequence of checks that the JVM goes through when determining how to handle an uncaught exception:

1. Check for a thread-specific handler to invoke, and if one exists, invoke it.

2. Invoke the handler of the containing ThreadGroup.

3. If the containing ThreadGroup (and its ancestors) have not overridden uncaughtException( ), pass the exception up the ThreadGroup hierarchy, until the root ThreadGroup is reached.

4. Invoke the default handler, obtained by calling Thread.getDefaultExceptionHandler( ).

Using Thread-Safe Collections

If you've ever used Java's collection classes in an environment with lots of threads, you know that Sun's nod to threading and collections is a bit heavy-handed. You can either use HashMap, List implementations, and Set implementations, which aren't thread-safe, and deal with threading on your own, or you can use Hashtable or Vector, which has synchronized methods all over the place. Tiger has added a number of thread-safe collections, many of which perform even better than Hashtable and Vector when used correctly. While these classes are hardly magic bullets, they offer more variety, and that's always a good thing.

How do I do that?

It's still beyond me why the read methods on Hashtable are synchronized.

All of Java's new concurrency support for collections is tucked away in java.util.concurrent. And, thankfully, the classes that mirror existing collections serve as drop-in replacements for their non-threadsafe counterparts.

ConcurrentHashMap

The first, and probably most valuable, collection to look at is java.util. concurrent.ConcurrentHashMap. This class makes the obvious first nod towards concurrence by *not* synchronizing any of its read methods. That takes care of a lot of locking and threading issues right off the bat. Even more importantly, ConcurrentHashMap segments its internal hashtable, so you can write to one segment while another thread writes to another (in addition to reads always being allowed). In terms of use, it is *identical* to HashMap, so you can add the following import:

```
import java.util.concurrent.ConcurrentHashMap;
```

Now all you have to do is search and replace on "HashMap," and you're all set. I won't bore you with the details...you should get the idea. Just make the change, and your code gets all the benefits of concurrent reads, and even concurrent writes most of the time.

CopyOnWriteArrayList

java.util.concurrent.CopyOnWriteArrayList is a thread-aware version of List, and particular (of course) ArrayList. This is a great solution for arrays that are updated infrequently, but are read very often. It disposes of synchronization, allowing any number of concurrent reads. For writing, it actually creates a new copy of the underlying array, and then assigns that new copy (with changes) back to the underlying copy.

CopyOnWriteArraySet

java.util.concurrent.CopyOnWriteArraySet works just like CopyOnWriteArrayList, and the same functionality applies. You get concurrent reading, and pay a fairly minimal performance cost, as long as you're reading a lot more than you are writing.

What just happened?

ConcurrentHashMap's magic is all in the segmentation of its internal hashtable. By default, there are 16 segments in this hashmap, and any operation on one segment has *no* effect on the others—including threading concerns. So you could, theoretically, have 16 threads operating on 16 different segments, all at the same time. If you have specialized needs for segmentation, you can specify the estimated threads that will write to the object:

```
Map map = new ConcurrentHashMap(2000, 25, 25);
```

The first parameter is the initial size, common to normal `HashMap` implementations. Next comes the load factor, and then the concurrency level. This isn't specifically named as the number of segments, but instead as the number of threads you expect to be performing concurrent updates. The implementation is then free to perform segmentation and internal sizing based upon that value.

As for the `CopyOnWrite` collections, you're basically getting around concurrency issues altogether. The reading part is easy—let any thread read from the collection anytime. Writing is a little trickier, and it's here where the downside comes into play. These collections create entirely new lists (or sets) on update, make the changes requested, and then the modified list (or set) is assigned to the instance. This is a pretty clumsy operation if you're doing lots of writes, but for an occasional write compared to a ton of reads, it works great, and you get a very fast, thread-aware (albeit not thread-safe) collection.

What about...

...the other classes and interfaces in `java.util.concurrent`? Many of these classes are covered in later labs, such as "Using Blocking Queues" and "Scheduling Tasks". But, there are some additional collection-analogs like those discussed here, such as `ConcurrentLinkedQueue`. Once you understand the basics presented here, you can figure out how these extra classes work with a quick glance at the Javadoc. Remember, most of these are drop-in substitutions for non-concurrent collections, so your learning curve should be next to nothing.

You also might be wondering about how these new classes work with iterators. Any `Iterator` instance obtained from `CopyOnWriteArrayList` and `CopyOnWriteArraySet` reflects the contents of the list or set *when it was obtained*. This means that you are essentially getting a snapshot of the list or set, rather than a dynamic version. Depending on your application, this can be absolutely great, or incredibly difficult! In general, use your iterators and ditch them, obtaining a new instance (through `iterator()`) if you need it again later. This will minimize the possibility of using stale data in your program logic.

Using Blocking Queues

In Chapter 1, you saw that Tiger introduced a new collection type, `java.util.Queue`. This interface has several implementations, such as `DelayQueue` and `PriorityQueue`. However, all of these assume sufficient room in the queue for adding elements, or, at the least, an error when there isn't room available.

True queues, though, often involve a wait period, where an element (or person—think of a line for a concert) waits in place until an opening is available. The same is true for removal—another thread (or unruly ticket-buyer) shouldn't be able to jump in front if there are already threads waiting to peel off the next item in the queue. Fortunately, the guys at Sun realized this is an important threading concept (or maybe just spent a lot of time trying to see Dave Matthews recently). In either case, the end-result is java.util.concurrent.BlockingQueue. This interface defines a means of blocking other threads on a put, or a take. As an added bonus, I'll even drop the concert ticket analogy now.

How do I do that?

The Queue interface defines the offer( ) method for adding elements to the queue, and the poll( ) method for removing elements. offer( ) should be used instead of add( ) (defined in Collection), because it returns a boolean value indicating if the addition was successful (implying that the queue was not full). In the same fashion, poll( ) simply returns null if the queue is empty. However, neither of these methods wait for space to be available, or for an element to be available, respectively.

"add( )" throws an unchecked exception if the queue is full, which isn't really appropriate, as a full queue isn't an exceptional condition.

java.util.concurrent.BlockingQueue is an interface that extends Queue, and adds two more methods: put( ) and take( ). This is one of those cases where a code sample is worth a thousand words, so take a look at Example 10-3. This represents one of the classic uses of a queue, in a producer/consumer relationship.

Example 10-3. A producer for a BlockingQueue

```
package com.oreilly.tiger.ch10;

import java.io.PrintStream;
import java.util.Date;
import java.util.concurrent.BlockingQueue;

public class Producer extends Thread {

  private BlockingQueue q;
  private PrintStream out;

  public Producer(BlockingQueue q, PrintStream out) {
    setName("Producer");
    this.q = q;
```

Example 10-3. *A producer for a BlockingQueue (continued)*

```
      this.out = out;
    }

    public void run() {
      try {
        while (true) {
          q.put(produce());
        }
      } catch (InterruptedException e) {
        out.printf("%s interrupted: %s", getName(), e.getMessage());
      }
    }

    private String produce() {
      while (true) {
        double r = Math.random();

        // Only goes forward 1/10 of the time
        if ((r*100) < 10) {
          String s = String.format("Inserted at %tc", new Date());
          return s;
        }
      }
    }
}
```

Example 10-4 is the consumer half of the relationship.

Example 10-4. *Consumer for a BlockingQueue*

```
package com.oreilly.tiger.ch10;

import java.io.PrintStream;
import java.util.concurrent.BlockingQueue;

public class Consumer extends Thread {

  private BlockingQueue q;
  private PrintStream out;

  public Consumer(String name, BlockingQueue q,
                  PrintStream out) {
    setName(name);
    this.q = q;
    this.out = out;
  }

  public void run() {
    try {
      while (true) {
        process(q.take());
      }
```

Example 10-4. Consumer for a BlockingQueue (continued)

```
    } catch (InterruptedException e) {
      out.printf("%s interrupted: %s", getName(), e.getMessage());
    }
  }

  private void process(Object obj) {
    out.printf("%s processing object:%n          '%s'%n",
               getName(), obj.toString());  }
}
```

Finally, here's a sample usage:

```
public void testQueue(PrintStream out) throws IOException {
  BlockingQueue queue = new LinkedBlockingQueue(10);
  Producer p = new Producer(queue, out);
  Consumer c1 = new Consumer("Consumer 1", queue, out);
  Consumer c2 = new Consumer("Consumer 2", queue, out);
  Consumer c3 = new Consumer("Consumer 3", queue, out);
  Consumer c4 = new Consumer("Consumer 4", queue, out);

  p.start(); c1.start(); c2.start(); c3.start(); c4.start();
  while (true) {
    // hang out for a while
  }
}
```

You can test out this method by running "ant run-ch10". It will wait forever, though, so you'll have to break out of the program.

You'll see tons of output, as the producer fills the queue and the consumers grab information out of it. What's cool, though, is that the processing cycles through the four consumers, in order:

```
[java] Consumer 1 processing object:
[java]          'Inserted at Tue May 04 08:43:50 GMT-06:00 2004'
[java] Consumer 2 processing object:
[java]          'Inserted at Tue May 04 08:43:50 GMT-06:00 2004'
[java] Consumer 3 processing object:
[java]          'Inserted at Tue May 04 08:43:50 GMT-06:00 2004'
[java] Consumer 4 processing object:
[java]          'Inserted at Tue May 04 08:43:50 GMT-06:00 2004'
[java] Consumer 1 processing object:
[java]          'Inserted at Tue May 04 08:43:50 GMT-06:00 2004'
[java] Consumer 2 processing object:
[java]          'Inserted at Tue May 04 08:43:50 GMT-06:00 2004'
[java] Consumer 3 processing object:
[java]          'Inserted at Tue May 04 08:43:50 GMT-06:00 2004'
[java] Consumer 4 processing object:
[java]          'Inserted at Tue May 04 08:43:50 GMT-06:00 2004'
```

It's a bit of luck that these came out in order. Your results may be completely different, order-wise.

This lets you know that each consumer, once it gets its turn, has a lock on the queue until it gets an object. This could take a few seconds, or a few days, and the threads really don't care.

There are five out-of-the-box implementations of BlockingQueue; all are in the java.util.concurrent package:

ArrayBlockingQueue

You have to specify the initial capacity when you create this queue, and like any other array, this capacity is the fixed limit. This queue has a somewhat reduced throughput as compared to other implementations, but threads are served in the order that they arrive.

LinkedBlockingQueue

This queue is based on a linked list (duh!). While you can specify a maximum size, it is by default unbounded.

There's a non-blocking version of PriorityBlocking-Queue, java.util. PriorityQueue.

PriorityBlockingQueue

This queue bases ordering on a specified Comparator, and the element returned by any take( ) call is the smallest element based on this ordering. If you don't specify a Comparator, the natural ordering is used (assuming the objects supplied to it implement Comparable). If your objects *don't* implement Comparable, and you don't have a Comparator to supply, there's really no reason to use PriorityBlockingQueue.

DelayQueue

DelayQueue is essentially a version of PriorityBlockingQueue that uses elements that implement the new java.util.concurrent. Delayed interface. Since this interface extends Comparable, it fits right into a PriorityBlockingQueue structure. Additionally, it won't allow an element to be grabbed with take( ) until that element's delay has elapsed.

If you're familiar at all with Ada (a programming language used most often in military defense programs), Synchronous-Queue is a lot like a rendezvous channel.

SynchronousQueue

This queue has a size of zero (yes, you read that correctly). It blocks put( ) calls until another thread calls take( ), and blocks take( ) calls until another thread calls put( ). Essentially, elements can only go directly from a producer to a consumer, and nothing is stored in the queue itself (other than for transition purposes).

These are self-explanatory, so pick the one you need, and go forth and code (well, after reading the rest of this chapter).

Specifying Timeouts for Blocking

When you're working with threads, you've often got to deal with blocking issues. Sometimes you may want to simply have a thread pause for a bit; other times you may be willing to wait, say, 10 seconds for an object lock, and then you'd rather move on than keep waiting. In these cases, it's possible to specify the exact time you want to wait using the new java.util.concurrent.TimeUnit enum.

How do I do that?

Tiger introduces the java.util.concurrent.TimeUnit enum, which defines four values: SECONDS, MILLISECONDS, MICROSECONDS, and NANOSECONDS. I'll even bet you've already figured out what this class does—it represents time, in meaningful units. One of the common uses is to put a thread to sleep for a specific amount of time:

```
try {
    TimeUnit.SECONDS.sleep(30);
} catch (InterruptedException e) {
    // report error
}
```

It's also common to use these units in specifying how long threads should want for locks, as in Blocking Queue.poll().

Here's an updated version of the testQueue( ) method, shown in "Using Blocking Queues":

```
public void testQueue(PrintStream out) throws IOException {
    BlockingQueue queue = new LinkedBlockingQueue( );
    Producer p = new Producer(queue, out);
    Consumer c1 = new Consumer("Consumer 1", queue, out);
    Consumer c2 = new Consumer("Consumer 2", queue, out);
    Consumer c3 = new Consumer("Consumer 3", queue, out);
    Consumer c4 = new Consumer("Consumer 4", queue, out);

    p.start(); c1.start(); c2.start(); c3.start(); c4.start();
    try {
      TimeUnit.SECONDS.sleep(2);
    } catch (InterruptedException ignored) { }
}
```

This enum defines several other methods of interest:

long convert(long duration, TimeUnit unit)
Converts the specified direction to units for the current TimeUnit.

Enums and defining custom methods are all covered in Chapter 3.

void sleep(long timeout)
Puts the thread to sleep for specified units (covered in this lab).

void timedJoin(Thread t, long duration)
Joins the supplied thread, as with t.join( ), with a timeout that once exceeded causes this process to bail out.

void timedWait(Object o, long duration)
Waits to get the lock on o for the specified duration.

toMicros( ), toMillis( ), toNanos( ), toSeconds( )

These are all conversion methods that take a long value for duration, and return a long value representing the converted value. These are all convenience versions of convert( ).

What about...

...statically importing TimeUnit? Yup, that's a good idea:

```
import static java.util.concurrent.TimeUnit.*;
```

Now you can write code like this:

```
try {
    SECONDS.sleep(2);
} catch (InterruptedException ignored) { }
```

Separating Thread Logic from Execution Logic

Suppose you've just spent 6 or 7 hours, heads-down, coming up with 10 or 15 complicated threads, many of which are interdependent, and finally have the queuing, ordering, and timing all figured out. Just as you're about to pop the top on a Coke™, your boss comes storming in, asking for more functionality, and you realize you're going to need to add another thread. While that in itself isn't hard, fitting them into the timing of the other threads is, and suddenly, you're looking at a complete redesign.

This is all too familiar for programmers working in multithreaded environments. The problem is that in Java (at least, pre–Tiger Java), threads' execution cycles are tied to the code they actually perform. Functionality and timing are all tied together. If you've got Tiger, though, you can get around this, and separate thread functionality from thread execution.

How do I do that?

One of the coolest new interfaces in the java.util.concurrent package is Executor. This interface defines a means of supplying threads to an object (which implements the Executor interface), and letting that object deal with timing and running of the threads, rather than forcing you to place this logic in your threading class. You add your Runnable objects to the Executor (which generally adds them to an internal queue), and the Executor then uses its own threads to peel off the objects and run them.

While you can create your own implementations of this class, you're better off using one of the pre-built implementations. These are not classes unto themselves, but pre-configured `Executor` implementations, each returned from a factory method on the `java.util.concurrent.Executors` class. Here's the basic rundown:

Single thread executor

Obtained with `Executors.newSingleThreadExecutor()`, this results in a pool size of 1, so tasks are executed one at a time.

Fixed thread executor

Obtained with `Executors.newFixedThreadPool(int poolSize)`, this creates an executor with the specified number of threads to run the tasks with which you supply it.

Cached thread executor

This executor, obtained with `Executors.newCachedThreadPool()`, will use as many threads as it needs to run the objects in its queue. It will reuse threads as they become available, as well as create new threads.

Scheduled thread executor

This executor is obtained with `Executors.newScheduledThreadPool()`, or `Executors.newSingleThreadScheduledExecutor()`, and is detailed in the "Executing Tasks Without an ExecutorService" section.

So what happens when you have just one little `Callable` object that you want to execute, and you don't need the overhead of `ExectorService`? Well, it seems those Sun guys thought of everything (except perhaps open-sourcing Java)—you use `FutureTask`.

How do I do that?

`java.util.concurrent.FutureTask` can be wrapped around `Callable` objects, allowing them to behave like a `Future` implementation returned from `ExecutorService.submit()`. The syntax is similar as well:

```
FutureTask<BigInteger> task =
    new FutureTask<BigInteger>(new RandomPrimeSearch(512));

new Thread(task).start();

BigInteger result = task.get();
```

The methods available to `FutureTask` are similar to `Future`, so I'll leave it to you to check out the Javadoc. With the details from "Using Callable Objects," you shouldn't have any problems.

What about...

...good old Runnable? Fortunately, plain old Thread and Runnable didn't get left out of the mix. You can wrap a FutureTask around a Runnable object just as easily as you can around a Callable object, and the same functionality applies. However, since Runnable's run( ) method doesn't return a result, the constructor is a bit different:

```
FutureTask<String> task =
    new FutureTask<String>(new MyRunnableObject, "Success!");
```

You have to supply a value to the constructor, of the type specified by your parameterization (in this example, a String), which is returned by get( ) if execution is successful. While the above example is valid, there are really only two common variants when using Runnable FutureTasks:

```
FutureTask<Object> task = new FutureTask<Object>(runnable, null);
```

```
FutureTask<Boolean> task = new FutureTask<Boolean>(runnable, true);
```

The first allows for discarding the result of get( ) altogether, and the second provides a true/false check for the result of get( ). You'd do well to use one of these yourself.

You essentially just create an Executor, give it some tasks, and then don't worry about it:

```
Executor e = Executors.newFixedThreadPool(5);

e.execute(new RunnableTask1( ));
e.execute(new RunnableTask2( ));
e.execute(new RunnableTask3( ));
```

I realize this goes against the nature of control freaks (of which I am one), but the Executor is quite competent to handle the running of your tasks.

Using Executor as a Service

While Executor on its own is a great addition to Java, there are times when you need more control over how execution occurs, when it stops, and even *how* it stops. For all of these cases, ExecutorService should be used.

How do I do that?

If you take a close look at the factory method signatures for Executors, you'll note that each returns an ExecutorService, rather than an Executor. java.util.concurrent.ExecutorService is a subinterface of Executor, and adds a good deal of functionality to the simple execute( ) method you saw in "Separating Thread Logic From Execution." Two of these are key in allowing you to stop an ExecutorService, either for an error condition or in a normal shutdown situation:

This isn't a fully (or even partially) functional FTP server, and is just used for example purposes. You won't find it in the sample code, as it doesn't actually work.

```java
public class FtpServer {

    private ExecutorService service;

    public FtpServer(int port) throws IOException {
        openSocket(port);
        service = Executors.newFixedThreadPool(100);
    }

    public void go() {
        try {
            while (true) {
                service.execute(new FtpHandler(getSocket()));
            }
        } catch (Exception e) {
            service.shutdownNow();
        }
    }

    public void stop() {
        try {
            service.shutdown();
        } catch (Exception e) {
            // report problem
        }
    }
}

class FtpHandler implements Runnable {

    private Socket socket;

    public FtpHandler(Socket socket) {
        this.socket = socket;
    }

    public void run() {
        // Handle connection
    }
}
```

Basically, getSocket( ) would wait for a client to connect, and return the connection to that client as a Socket object.

This little pseudo-class primarily illustrates two methods:

shutdown( )

> This method stop the service, but first allows the service to attempt to complete all running and queued tasks. No new tasks are accepted after this call, though.

shutdownNow( )

> A little more direct, this method stops the service, and does *not* allow any queued or running tasks to execute. Currently running tasks are basically tossed, and queued tasks are returned via a List<Runnable>, for program use (if desired—in the example, I ignored these completely).

You can choose whichever of these suits you, based on your application needs. There's one other big advantage of using ExecutorService, which the next lab, "Using Callable Objects," looks at in detail.

Using Callable Objects

Java's Thread class has been around for a while, and certainly stood the test of time. However, there are a few things that Thread's run( ) method can't do—one is to throw checked Exceptions (exceptions from run( ) are not checked at compile time), and the other is to return a result. Both of these are things that you can get around with some clever programming, but in Tiger, you no longer have to. Instead, use the new java.util. concurrent.Callable class.

How do I do that?

An object that implements the Callable interface only needs to implement one method: call( ). The interface is a generic type, and the parameter you supply to the interface is the type returned by call( ). So the call( ) method for a class that implements Callable<String> returns a String.

Like Thread's run( ) method, you can invoke call( ) directly—but it's better to let an ExecutorService handle execution, by passing it to the submit( ) method of ExecutorService. Let's put these concepts to work, so you can get a better idea of how this fits together. Example 10-5 is a Callable implementation that computes random prime numbers.

Thanks to David Flanagan for another nice bit of example code.

Example 10-5. A Callable implementation

```
package com.oreilly.tiger.ch10;

import java.math.BigInteger;
import java.security.SecureRandom;
import java.util.Random;
import java.util.concurrent.Callable;


public class RandomPrimeSearch implements Callable<BigInteger> {

  private static final Random prng = new SecureRandom( );
  private int bitSize;

  public RandomPrimeSearch(int bitSize) {
    this.bitSize = bitSize;
  }

  public BigInteger call( ) {
    return BigInteger.probablePrime(bitSize, prng);
  }
}
```

Now you can pass one or more of these objects to submit( ):

```
ExecutorService service = Executors.newFixedThreadPool(5);
Future<BigInteger> prime1 = service.submit(new RandomPrimeSearch(512));
Future<BigInteger> prime2 = service.submit(new RandomPrimeSearch(512));
Future<BigInteger> prime3 = service.submit(new RandomPrimeSearch(512));
```

This should all make sense, except for the addition of a new class: java. util.concurrent.Future. Here's the deal: like a Thread, a Callable object runs happily in the background, and your application won't wait for it to finish. However, as call( ) returns a value, there has to be a way to obtain that value, without having to have it right away (and forcing your program to wait around). This is where Future comes in—it allows you to operate upon the Callable object, including getting the value of call( ) and stopping its execution, without causing your entire program to block. Here are the methods of Future you want to be familiar with:

boolean cancel (boolean mayInterruptIfRunning)
    This attempts to cancel execution of the task. If the task has not started, it is cancelled; if it has started, mayInterruptIfRunning determines if it is cancelled.

V get( )
    This parameterized method returns the result of the task, waiting for completion if needed.

```
V get(long timeout, TimeUnit unit)
```
This parameterized method returns the result of the task, if it completes within the specified waiting period.

```
boolean isCancelled( )
```
This indicates if the task was cancelled before normal completion.

```
boolean isDone( )
```
This indicates if the task is complete.

In most cases, you'll simply call get( ) and wait for the result:

```
ExecutorService service = Executors.newFixedThreadPool(5);
Future<BigInteger> prime1 = service.submit(new RandomPrimeSearch(512));
Future<BigInteger> prime2 = service.submit(new RandomPrimeSearch(512));
Future<BigInteger> prime3 = service.submit(new RandomPrimeSearch(512));

try {
  BigInteger bigger = (prime1.get( ).multiply(prime2.get( ))).
multiply(prime3.get( ));
  out.println(bigger);
} catch (InterruptedException e) {
  e.printStackTrace(out);
} catch (ExecutionException e) {
  e.printStackTrace(out);
}
```

You don't need to call isDone( ) and then call get( ); get( ) will wait for a completed result before returning.

The other methods are typically useful when you have more of a daemon and need to cleanly cancel or shut down tasks yet to be executed.

Executing Tasks Without an ExecutorService

So what happens when you just have one little Callable object that you want to execute, and you don't need the overhead of ExectorService? Well, it seems those Sun guys thought of everything (except perhaps open sourcing Java)—you use FutureTask.

How do I do that?

java.util.concurrent.FutureTask can be wrapped around Callable objects, allowing them to behave like a Future implementation returned from ExecutorService.submit( ). The syntax is similar as well:

```
FutureTask<BigInteger> task =
  new FutureTask<BigInteger>(new RandomPrimeSearch(512));

new Thread(task).start();

BigInteger result = task.get( );
```

The methods available to FutureTask are similar to Future, so I'll leave it to you to check out the Javadoc. With the details from "Using Callable Objects," you shouldn't have any problems.

What about...

...good old Runnable? Fortunately, plain old Thread and Runnable didn't get left out of the mix. You can wrap a FutureTask around a Runnable object just as easily as you can around a Callable object, and the same functionality applies. However, since Runnable's run( ) method doesn't return a result, the constructor is a bit different:

```
FutureTask<String> task =
    new FutureTask<String>(new MyRunnableObject, "Success!");
```

You have to supply a value to the constructor, of the type specified by your parameterization (in this example, a String), which is returned by get( ) if execution is successful. While the above example is valid, there are really only two common variants when using Runnable FutureTasks:

```
FutureTask<Object> task = new FutureTask<Object>(runnable, null);

FutureTask<Boolean> task = new FutureTask<Boolean>(runnable, true);
```

The first allows for discarding the result of get( ) altogether, and the second provides a true/false check for the result of get( ). You'd do well to use one of these yourself.

Scheduling Tasks

Along with the ability to separate the logic of a task (in a Callable, Runnable, or Thread object) from its execution, Tiger allows you to schedule execution at specific times.

How do I do that?

Earlier, you saw how the Executors class was used to obtain several ExecutorServices. Two methods that were brushed over were newScheduledThreadPool( ) and newSingleThreadScheduledExecutor( ). Both of these return instances of ScheduledExecutorService, which adds several features to the basic ExecutorService interface. The simplest to use is scheduleAtFixedRate( ), shown in action in Example 10-6.

Example 10-6. Using scheduled tasks

```java
package com.oreilly.tiger.ch10;

import java.io.IOException;
import java.io.PrintStream;
import java.util.Date;
import java.util.concurrent.Executors;
import java.util.concurrent.ScheduledExecutorService;
import java.util.concurrent.ScheduledFuture;

import static java.util.concurrent.TimeUnit.*;

public class ScheduleTester {

  public static void main(String[] args) {
    // Get the scheduler
    ScheduledExecutorService scheduler =
      Executors.newSingleThreadScheduledExecutor();

    // Get a handle, starting now, with a 10 second delay
    final ScheduledFuture<?> timeHandle =
    scheduler.scheduleAtFixedRate(new TimePrinter(System.out), 0, 10, SECONDS);

    // Schedule the event, and run for 1 hour (60 * 60 seconds)
    scheduler.schedule(new Runnable() {
      public void run() {
        timeHandle.cancel(false);
      }
    }, 60*60, SECONDS);

    }
  }
}

class TimePrinter implements Runnable {

  private PrintStream out;

  public TimePrinter(PrintStream out) {
    this.out = out;
  }

  public void run() {
    out.printf("Current time: %tr%n", new Date());
  }
}
```

Here's some output from this class:

```
[echo] Running ScheduleTester...
[java] Current time: 09:17:04 AM
[java] Current time: 09:17:14 AM
[java] Current time: 09:17:24 AM
[java] Current time: 09:17:34 AM
```

This code is actually every bit as simple as it looks. You obtain a new ScheduledExecutorService from Executors, and use the scheduleAtFixedRate() method to initiate a task. This method takes the task to run (either a Runnable or Callable implementation, then takes a delay (how long to wait before beginning execution), the period between executions, and the TimeUnit that these durations are expressed in. In the example, the TimePrinter thread is set up to run immediately, and then every 10 seconds thereafter.

The scheduleAtFixedRate() method returns a ScheduledFuture instance, which extends both the Future interface (detailed in "Using Callable Objects"), and the Delayed interface, which I haven't mentioned yet. Delayed is used for objects that are acted upon after a certain delay. Its getDelay() method, in the context of a ScheduledFuture, allows you to determine how much time is left before subsequent executions of your task.

The final piece of the puzzle is the schedule() invocation, which at first glance may confuse you. schedule() works just like scheduleAtFixedRate(), but sets up a single execution, rather than multiple ones. In the example, it's used to initiate a thread that will cancel the execution of TimePrinter, after an hour (60*60 seconds). This is an important part of scheduling—otherwise the thread printing the date would run on infinitely. It also makes the ScheduledFuture object important—it provides the only means of canceling the task's execution.

What about...

...that final declaration on the ScheduledFuture object? Because the inner class passed to the scheduler has to access the Future object, you've got to mark it as final. Otherwise, you'll get this error:

```
[javac] code\src\com\oreilly\tiger\ch10\ScheduleTester.java:26:
        local variable timeHandle is accessed from within inner class;
        needs to be declared final
[javac]         timeHandle.cancel(true);
[javac]         ^
[javac] 1 error
```

You'll run into this with all your scheduling programs, so you might want to keep this in mind.

For a lengthy discussion on the "final" keyword, you might want to check out Hardcore Java (O'Reilly).

Advanced Synchronizing

If you've not begun to spew out `syncrhonized` statements by this point in the chapter, you are probably the type of programmer that would be into the new synchronizers available in the `java.util.concurrent` package. Unfortunately, the intimate details are beyond this book (it's a notebook, not an encyclopedia); still, here are some basics to get you pointed in the right direction.

How do I do that?

Tiger introduces four *synchronizer* classes. They all allow you to force threads to wait for a specific condition before continuing execution:

Semaphore

All four of these classes are in the java.util.concurrent package.

The term *semaphore* has actually been around as long as concurrent programming. A semaphore represents one or more permits. Threads call `acquire( )` to obtain a permit from the semaphore, and `release( )` when done with the permit. If no permits are available, `acquire( )` blocks, waiting for one to become available. In other words, a semaphore acts like a bouncer, only allowing so many people into the party at one time.

Variants on `acquire( )`, which allow some control over what happens when a block is encountered, include `tryAcquire( )`, which either never blocks or blocks for a specified timeout, and `acquireUninterruptibly( )`, which won't let go even if an `InterruptionException` occurs.

CountDownLatch

A `CountDownLatch` is used to block threads until a certain set of operations is complete. When a latch is created, it is closed—any thread that calls the latch's `await( )` method will block until the latch is opened. This allows threads to wait on the latch, ensuring that all operations are complete before continuing.

Threads that are performing those required operations can call `countDown( )` to decrement the counter supplied to a `CountDownLatch` at its construction. When the latch's counter reaches O, the latch opens, and all threads sitting in `await( )` become unblocked and continue execution.

Exchanger

An `Exchanger` provides for thread rendezvous for two threads, typically in a consumer-producer relationship. At some point these threads must "synch up," and possibly exchange the results of their individual tasks.

The most common use of an Exchanger is when a producer fills a buffer with data, and a consumer drains data from another source. Once the producer has filled its buffer, and the consumer drained its buffer, the two can swap buffers, and continue operation. However, *both* threads must complete their tasks before swapping. Exchanger. exchange( ) does the work here, as you might expect.

CyclicBarrier

CyclicBarrier is another thread rendezvous facility. However, this handles the case where multiple threads (generally more than two) must *all* rendezvous at a specified point. You specify the number of threads when you create the barrier, and then each thread calls await( ) when it reaches the point where it's ready to rendezvous. That blocks the thread until all related threads reach the barrier.

Once all the threads have called await( ), the blocking stops, and all the threads can continue (and often interact). Additionally, the barrier is all-or-none: if one thread fails abnormally, and leaves a barrier point prematurely, all threads leave abnormally.

All of these are covered in detail in the newest edition of *Java Threads* (O'Reilly), which should be showing up on bookshelves in mid- to late-summer, 2004. If you're into mutexes, semaphores, and latches, that's the place to go. They'll also be covered in the upcoming *Java in a Nutshell,* Fifth Edition (O'Reilly).

Using Atomic Types

Another advanced threading feature introduced in Tiger is that of *atomic type.* An *atomic operation* is one that is indivisible: no other threads can interrupt or examine a variable in the middle of an atomic operation. There's the beginning state, the end state, and (for all other threads) nothing in between. An atomic type is simply a type that has atomic operations available to it—it manages to be thread-safe despite being essentially lock-free.

How do I do that?

All atomic types are defined in the java.util.concurrent.atomic package. There are a number of types, revolving around Boolean, Long, Integer, and object references. This allows you to perform atomic operations on these types, using AtomicBoolean, AtomicLong, AtomicInteger, and AtomicReference, respectively.

There are some variations on these types, with additional features, that you can check out in the Tiger Javadocs.

Each type provides a get() and set() method, which do what you would expect (get and set the type's value, using an atomic operation). They also offer getAndSet( ), which sets the value, returning the previous value, as well as compareAndSet( ), which checks the value, and if it matches the supplied value, sets it to a new value. Additionally, AtomicInteger and AtomicLong provide for atomic versions of ++ and --, through variations on decrement( ) and increment( ) methods. For example, decrementAndGet( ) decrements the value of the atomic type, and returns the update value; getAndIncrement( ) returns the current value, and then increments it in the type. Here are several different ways to write a thread-safe counter, lifted straight out of *Java in a Nutshell*, Fifth Edition (O'Reilly):

"compareAndSet" is the canonical atomic operation.

```
// Rely on locking to prevent concurrent access
int count1 = 0;
public synchronized int count1( ) {
  return count1++;
}

// Rely on the atomic operations to prevent concurrent access
AtomicInteger count2 = new AtomicInteger(0);
public int count2( ) {
  return count2.getAndIncrement( );
}

// Optimistic locking -- compare the result, to minimize overhead,
//    and only correct if needed
AtomicInteger count3 = new AtomicInteger(0);
public int count3( ) {
  int result;
  do {
    result = count3.get( );
  } while (!count3.compareAndSet(result, result+1));
  return result;
}
```

If you're not familiar with object references, it's simply the reference to an object. AtomicReference, then, allows you to work with an object atomically, by getting and setting the reference in an indivisible manner. The most useful method on AtomicReference is probably compareAndSet( ), which lets you change an object reference if it doesn't match the supplied value.

Like the lab "Advanced Synchronizing," getting too much further into atomic types would have us well into the ground covered by *Java Threads* (O'Reilly), so I'll refer you to that work if you need to get further detail on atomic types.

What about...

...types like byte, short, and char? These (and their wrapper types) can all be stored in an AtomicInteger, providing you the same functionality. You'll just have to do a little conversion on the object's return values, which are almost always an int.

You can also use these atomic operations on arrays of the Integer, Long, and reference types (but not Boolean). java.util.concurrent. atomic defines AtomicIntegerArray, AtomicLongArray, and AtomicReferenceArray for just these occasions. They provide all the methods of their non-array counterparts, but each method takes an int index to indicate which item in the array you want to operate upon.

Locking Versus Synchronization

The final topic I want to address is the new Lock interface that Tiger provides, along with its companion interface, Condition. If you're happy using the synchronized keyword, then this section might not really interest you. However, if you find synchronized limiting, using Lock might solve your problems.

How do I do that?

Tiger introduces the java.util.concurrent.locks package to add more flexible and extensive locking than available with the synchronized keyword. At its simplest, the Lock class can be made to emulate a synchronized block by calling lock( ), and then unlock( ) when done. However, it's in going beyond these basics that things get interesting.

Lock provides a lockInterruptibly( ) method, which obtains a lock but allows for interruptions—this is something a synchronized block can't offer. There are also tryLock( ) methods that attempt to get a lock, but will not wait (or will wait for a specified duration)—another feature not available through use of a synchronized block. If a thread is waiting for a lock on a synchronized method or code block, it will happily (and quietly) wait forever.

To add to the fun, the java.util.concurrent.locks.Condition interface provides for multiple wait-sets per object. This allows conditions to keep threads waiting, and for releasing threads from a wait state based on specific (and even multiple) conditions. So a thread waiting to write, and only then if a value is changed, can be handled differently than a thread that is waiting to write without needing a value to be changed.

Can you tell David Flanagan helped out a lot on this chapter? Thanks, David!

Example 10-7 (borrowed from *Java in a Nutshell*, Fifth Edition (O'Reilly)) demonstrates the most common use of explicit locking, something called *hand-over-hand locking*. In this scenario, a linked list is used: a lock is obtained on one node, and then the next node, and traversed one node at a time. However, at each stage, the prior node is released, so only two nodes (at most) in the list are ever locked at once. There's simply no way to simulate this functionality without explicit locking.

Example 10-7. Contrived linked list example

```
package com.oreilly.tiger.ch10;
```

As David points out in Java in a Nutshell, this is a pretty useless list, functionally, although it's a great example.

```
import java.util.concurrent.locks.Condition;
import java.util.concurrent.locks.Lock;
import java.util.concurrent.locks.ReentrantLock;

public class LinkList<E> {

  // The value of this node
  E value;

  // The rest of the list
  LinkList<E> rest;

  // A lock for this node
  Lock lock;

  // Signals when the value of this node changes
  Condition valueChanged;

  // Signals when the node this is connected to changes
  Condition linkChanged;

  public LinkList(E value) {
    this.value = value;
    rest = null;
    lock = new ReentrantLock();
    valueChanged = lock.newCondition();
    linkChanged = lock.newCondition();
  }
```

Example 10-7. Contrived linked list example (continued)

```
public void setValue(E value) {
  lock.lock();
  try {
    this.value = value;

    // Let waiting threads that the value has changed
    valueChanged.signalAll();
  } finally {
    lock.unlock();
  }
}

public void executeOnValue(E desiredValue, Runnable task)
  throws InterruptedException {

  lock.lock();
  try {
    // Checks the value against the desired value
    while (!value.equals(desiredValue)) {
      // This will wait until the value changes
      valueChanged.await();
    }

    // When we get here, the value is correct -- Run the task
    task.run();
  } finally {
    lock.unlock();
  }
}

public void append(E value) {
  // Start the pointer at this node
  LinkList<E> node = this;
  node.lock.lock();

  while (node.rest != null) {
    LinkList<E> next = node.rest;

    // Here's the hand-over-hand locking
    try {
      // Lock the next node
      next.lock.lock();
    } finally {
      // unlock the current node
      node.lock.unlock();
    }

    // Traverse
    node = next;
  }
```

Example 10-7. *Contrived linked list example (continued)*

```
        // We're at the final node, so append and then unlock
        try {
            node.rest = new LinkList<E>(value);

            // Let any waiting threads know that this node's link has changed
            node.linkChanged.signalAll();
        } finally {
            node.lock.unlock();
        }
    }

    public void printUntilInterrupted(String prefix) {
        // Start the pointer at this node
        LinkList<E> node = this;
        node.lock.lock();

        while (true) {
            LinkList<E> next;
            try {
                System.out.println(prefix + ": " + node.value);

                // Wait for the next node if not available
                while (node.rest == null) {
                    node.linkChanged.await();
                }

                // Get the next node
                next = node.rest;

                // Lock it - more hand-to-hand locking
                next.lock.lock();
            } catch (InterruptedException e) {
                // reset the interrupt status
                Thread.currentThread().interrupt();
                return;
            } finally {
                node.lock.unlock();
            }

            // Traverse
            node = next;
        }
    }
}
```

If you can use synchronized blocks or methods instead of an explicit Lock object, you don't have to worry about unlocking; Java takes care of it for you.

Take special notice that you never see a call to lock() without an immediate try/finally bock in which unlock() is called. This is something you need to lock (no pun intended) into your own head—otherwise you'll eventually make a mistake somewhere, and leave an object infinitely locked.

Chapter 10: Threading

The rest of the code turns out to be pretty straightforward. Walk through it slowly, and I trust you'll have a good overview of both the Lock and Condition interface.

What about...

...other types of locks? Tiger provides ReentrantLock (used in this code), which most closely approximates a synchronized block, albeit with the extra features of a Lock. Tiger also defines a ReadWriteLock, which maintains a separate lock for reading than for writing. Multiple threads may hold the read lock, as reading is typically a safe concurrent operation, but only one thread may hold the write lock. Implementations of this class (such as ReentrantReadWriteLock) are best used for large sets of data, where reading happens often and writing occurs for small sections of data.

Index

We'd like to hear your suggestions for improving our indexes. Send email to *index@oreilly.com*.

Colophon

Our look is the result of reader comments, our own experimentation, and feedback from distribution channels. Distinctive covers complement our distinctive approach to technical topics, breathing personality and life into potentially dry subjects.

The *Developer's Notebook* series is modeled on the tradition of laboratory notebooks. Laboratory notebooks are an invaluable tool for researchers and their successors.

The purpose of a laboratory notebook is to facilitate the recording of data and conclusions as the work is being conducted, creating a faithful and immediate history. The notebook begins with a title page that includes the owner's name and the subject of research. The pages of the notebook should be numbered and prefaced with a table of contents. Entries must be clear, easy to read, and accurately dated; they should use simple, direct language to indicate the name of the experiment and the steps taken. Calculations are written out carefully and relevant thoughts and ideas recorded. Each experiment is introduced and summarized as it is added to the notebook. The goal is to produce comprehensive, clearly organized notes that can be used as a reference. Careful documentation creates a valuable record and provides a practical guide for future developers.

Reg Aubry was the production editor and copyeditor for *Java 1.5 Tiger: A Developer's Notebook*. Sada Preisch was the proofreader. Sada Preisch, Colleen Gorman, and Claire Cloutier provided quality control. Johnna and Tom Dinse wrote the index.

Edie Freedman designed the cover of this book. Emma Colby produced the cover layout with QuarkXPress 4.1 using the Officina Sans and JuniorHandwriting fonts.

Melanie Wang designed the interior layout, based on a series design by Edie Freedman and David Futato. This book was converted by Julie Hawks to FrameMaker 5.5.6 with a format conversion tool created by Erik Ray, Jason McIntosh, Neil Walls, and Mike Sierra that uses Perl and XML technologies. The text font is Adobe Boton; the heading font is ITC Officina Sans; the code font is LucasFont's TheSans Mono Condensed, and the handwriting font is a modified version of JRHand made by Tepid Monkey Fonts and modified by O'Reilly. The illustrations that appear in the book were produced by Robert Romano and Jessamyn Read using Macromedia FreeHand 9 and Adobe Photoshop 6. This colophon was written by Colleen Gorman.

Need in-depth answers fast?

Access over 2,000 of the newest and best technology books online

Safari Bookshelf is the premier electronic reference library for IT professionals and programmers—a must-have when you need to pinpoint exact answers in an instant.

Access over 2,000 of the top technical reference books by twelve leading publishers including O'Reilly, Addison-Wesley, Peachpit Press, Prentice Hall, and Microsoft Press. Safari provides the technical references and code samples you need to develop quality, timely solutions.

Try it today with a FREE TRIAL
Visit *www.oreilly.com/safari/max/*

For groups of five or more, set up a free, 30-day corporate trial
Contact: *corporate@oreilly.com*

What Safari Subscribers Say:

"The online books make quick research a snap. I usually keep Safari up all day and refer to it whenever I need it."
—Joe Bennett, Sr. Internet Developer

"I love how Safari allows me to access new books each month depending on my needs. The search facility is excellent and the presentation is top notch. It is one heck of an online technical library."
—Eric Winslow, Economist-System,
Administrator-Web Master-Programmer

Related Titles Available from O'Reilly

Java

Ant: The Definitive Guide

Eclipse: A Java Developer's Guide

Enterprise JavaBeans, *3rd Edition*

Hardcore Java

Head First Java

Head First Servlets & JSP

Head First EJB

J2EE Design Patterns

Java and SOAP

Java & XML Data Binding

Java & XML

Java Cookbook

Java Data Objects

Java Database Best Practices

Java Enterprise Best Practices

Java Enterprise in a Nutshell, *2nd Edition*

Java Examples in a Nutshell, *3rd Edition*

Java Extreme Programming Cookbook

Java in a Nutshell, *4th Edition*

Java Management Extensions

Java Message Service

Java Network Programming, *2nd Edition*

Java NIO

Java Performance Tuning, *2nd Edition*

Java RMI

Java Security, *2nd Edition*

Java ServerPages, *2nd Edition*

Java Serlet & JSP Cookbook

Java Servlet Programming, *2nd Edition*

Java Swing, *2nd Edition*

Java Web Services in a Nutshell

Learning Java, *2nd Edition*

Mac OS X for Java Geeks

NetBeans: The Definitive Guide

Programming Jakarta Struts

Tomcat: The Definitive Guide

WebLogic: The Definitive Guide

O'REILLY®

Our books are available at most retail and online bookstores.
To order direct: 1-800-998-9938 • *order@oreilly.com* • *www.oreilly.com*
Online editions of most O'Reilly titles are available by subscription at *safari.oreilly.com*

Keep in touch with O'Reilly

1. Download examples from our books

To find example files for a book, go to:

www.oreilly.com/catalog

select the book, and follow the "Examples" link.

2. Register your O'Reilly books

Register your book at *register.oreilly.com*

Why register your books?
Once you've registered your O'Reilly books you can:

- Win O'Reilly books, T-shirts or discount coupons in our monthly drawing.
- Get special offers available only to registered O'Reilly customers.
- Get catalogs announcing new books (US and UK only).
- Get email notification of new editions of the O'Reilly books you own.

3. Join our email lists

Sign up to get topic-specific email announcements of new books and conferences, special offers, and O'Reilly Network technology newsletters at:

elists.oreilly.com

It's easy to customize your free elists subscription so you'll get exactly the O'Reilly news you want.

4. Get the latest news, tips, and tools

www.oreilly.com

- "Top 100 Sites on the Web"—PC Magazine
- CIO Magazine's Web Business 50 Awards

Our web site contains a library of comprehensive product information (including book excerpts and tables of contents), downloadable software, background articles, interviews with technology leaders, links to relevant sites, book cover art, and more.

5. Work for O'Reilly

Check out our web site for current employment opportunities:

jobs.oreilly.com

6. Contact us

O'Reilly & Associates
1005 Gravenstein Hwy North
Sebastopol, CA 95472 USA

TEL: 707-827-7000 or 800-998-9938
         (6am to 5pm PST)

FAX: 707-829-0104

order@oreilly.com
For answers to problems regarding your order or our products. To place a book order online, visit:

www.oreilly.com/order_new

catalog@oreilly.com
To request a copy of our latest catalog.

booktech@oreilly.com
For book content technical questions or corrections.

corporate@oreilly.com
For educational, library, government, and corporate sales.

proposals@oreilly.com
To submit new book proposals to our editors and product managers.

international@oreilly.com
For information about our international distributors or translation queries. For a list of our distributors outside of North America check out:

international.oreilly.com/distributors.html

adoption@oreilly.com
For information about academic use of O'Reilly books, visit:

academic.oreilly.com